OPTION TRADING

2 Books in 1:

The Complete guide for Beginners to learn Options Trading
and the best strategies quickly. Bonus Chapter for
Day Trading and Swing Trading are included, along
with the top mindset to look to your future concretely

Luke Rober

Table of Contents

Luke Rober

Luke Rober was born in New York City in 1988 and grew up in a middle-class family.

From a young age, he had a deep passion for numbers and the laws that govern them.

Before finishing his studies in mathematical engineering, he had already found a great job in a well-known international software and programming company as a data analyst.

After completing his studies, he dedicated himself entirely to his company's long and tedious work. Then, by chance, he discovered the magical world of trading and options a day.

Over time, he realized that trading is the future and is a winning way to make money while having fun.

At this point, he applied all his mathematical and logical knowledge to generate substantial extra income to his income and live a more peaceful and serene life.

Today he is happily living with his current partner near Manhattan, and in a few months, their family will expand.

Luke is thrilled with his life and the economic security he can pass on to his loved ones.

It is also possible to communicate with the author directly at this email address: **lukerober.options@outlook.com**

Luke will be happy to answer you even for a simple chat.

Enjoy reading

BOOK 1

OPTIONS TRADING FOR BEGINNERS

The Complete Guide Will Have You Generating your First Passive Income in No Time. Learn How the Basics Of The Most Profitable Investments Utilize Options Intelligently

"Price is what you pay, value is what you get."

W. Buffett

Introduction

Options trading is a way to gain exposure to movements in the price of an asset without having to own it outright. There's a good chance that your broker already has options trading accounts set up for you and they'll take care of all the paperwork and day-to-day stuff, but if you're interested in learning more about it, this intro will give you of what options are, how they work, how they can help with day trading and swing trading."

Many people think that trade options are just for rich Wall Street guys who take advantage of their money changing hands quickly. However, this isn't true at all. It's more likely that they know something about options and would be able to take advantage of it.

Day trading is the act of buying and selling securities within the same trading day. This form of trading is typically done by investors who are using automated traders, possibly over several days or weeks, with the goal of making money on both their short-term trades as well as timing larger market events that occur over longer periods. As a result, day traders typically use indicators like moving averages to time entries and exits.

Swing trading refers to an investor's attempts to make money through long position trades (purchasing shares or other financial instruments for the long-term), while hedging them with short positions (selling shares or other financial instruments for the short term) in order to minimize volatility. This form of trading is similar to day trading, in that position sizes are small, but differs because it takes multiple days or weeks before the position is closed. Swing traders are generally longer-term investors, who are not reacting to market forces in real time, but instead employ technical analysis to identify when security prices will reach certain values based on previous patterns. Also see Range trading

Some funds offer a combination of both day and swing elements. This is typically done with the intent of reducing overall portfolio volatility and lower portfolio turnover (i.e., reducing commissions).

The funds of the large investment banks whose employees tend to trade on the stock market during regular business hours are generally considered day traders. Other investment banks may also engage in day trading, but trade more through their overnight systems using algorithms that are not necessarily available to retail investors. This is particularly true of hedge funds that invest in derivatives or other highly speculative instruments.

Day trading is considered controversial among professional investors, who believe it is less profitable than longer term investing in which price movements are not dependent on human emotions. Some argue that this position is exaggerated by the media, which often covers volatility in market action as a form of entertainment rather than education. Others also argue that day trading is simply part of the evolution of markets (a natural process), and actually increases liquidity by spreading out buy and sell orders.

Nevertheless, it is generally accepted that day trading requires a considerable amount of capital (which may be one reason retail traders do not engage in day trading), as well as high levels of self-discipline. When done poorly, day trading can result in substantial financial losses to the investor within a relatively short period of time.

What are Options?

Options are a type of security with an expiration date and which gives the holder the right to buy or sell a specific quantity of an underlying asset. Let's say you want to invest in stocks, but want to wait for the "perfect" moment. Instead of buying, say, 100 shares of Apple at $200 per share today, you could buy one call contract on Apple instead for $2 per share. If Apple goes up past your break-even point, your call might be worth more than the initial investment. If it doesn't go up enough before expiration date you can let it expire worthless and never have to worry about it again.

Options were invented by John Vega in 1973. Vega's idea was to trade options on commodities based on other commodities. When Vega passed away in 1982, the futures industry took the idea and ran with it. Today there are plenty of calls, puts and futures-based options available, only some of which only go up in value while others only go down.

The amount needed to buy an option depends on whether you want to be long or short the underlying asset. Let's say you're looking to buy 100 shares of Apple (AAPL) at $200 per share today (the price is irrelevant but I'm assuming here). You'd need to come up with $20,000. That's the money you're risking that Apple won't go up enough for you to make a profit.

If instead you buy one call contract on Apple at $2 per share and it rises above $240 before expiration (in, say, three months), it would be worth somewhere around $5.50 per share. So, the 100 shares you get from exercising your call would only cost $1,850 [$240 - $2 = $238 x 100 = $23800 - 20,000 = $15800].

The difference between the price of your call and the price of the stock when you buy or sell an option is known as "option premium.

Agreed-Upon Price

Also known as the strike price. It does not change no matter how much time has passed, and it is so named because the trader strikes when the underlying value makes the desired income.

Specified Time

Also known as the expiration dates. This is the date at which the option (contract) expires. The trader can exercise the option at the strike price at any time up until the expiry date reaches. In some countries, such as Europe, a trader can only exercise the right to the option at the strike price exactly on the expiry date. We will more largely focus on the American way of trading options, which allows for exercising right on.

Rights Acquired with The Purchase of An Options

They can be call (right of purchase) and put (right of sale).

Trading options and trading stocks are different because stocks and options have different characteristics. Stocks stand for shares of ownership in individual companies or opportunities. It allows the stock trader to bet in any direction that they feel the stock price headed.

Stocks are an excellent investment if you think of long-term yields, such as for retirement and have the capital. They are very simplistic in the approach in that the trader buys the stock and wagers on the price they think will rise at a particular time in the future. The hope is that the price will increase in value, thus gaining the trader a substantial yield.

Stocks are an excellent option for those who want to invest without keeping a steady eye on the growth of the investment.

The risk of investing in stocks is that the price of shares can plummet to zero at any moment. It means that the investor can lose their entire investment at the drop of a hat because stocks are very volatile today. They are very reactive to world events such as wars, politics, scandals, epidemics, and natural disasters.

On the other hand, options are an excellent option for traders who would like flexibility with timing and risks. The trader is under no obligation and can see how the trade plays out over the time specified by the option contract. In that period, the price is locked, which is also a great appeal.

Trading options also require a lower investment compared to stocks typically.

Another excellent appeal for options trading is that the specified time is typically shorter than investing in stocks. For regular buying and selling as options have different expiration dates. Expiration dates extent from just a few days to several years.

The drawback that makes some people hesitate in trading options is that it is more complicated than trading stocks. The trader needs to learn new jargon and vocabulary such as strike prices, calls and puts to determine how they can set up effective options. Not only does the trader have to learn new terms, but they also have to develop new skillsets and the right mindset for options trading.

What Is Options Trading?

Options trading is where you buy, sell or trade the rights to buy or sell stocks in the future. Puts and calls are the two forms of options.

A put option allows you to sell a stock at a pre-determined price in the future.

You can buy a stock at a certain price in the future if you buy a call option. When we speak about Trading, we mean buying and selling of these rights (options) on an exchange such as NASDAQ, NYSE, BATS etc.

Puts are used when you are bearish on the market. You are then bullish on the price of the stock because you bought a put option with it. Calls are used when you are bullish on the market. You are then bearish on the price of the stock because you bought a call option with it.

Options As Derivatives

The options belong to the largest group of securities called derivatives. The price of one derivative depends on or is derived from the price of another. For example, wine is a grape derivative, ketchup is a tomato derivative, and a stock option is a stock derivative. Options are financial instrument derivatives—their interest depends on the price of another currency. Calls, puts, futures, forward, swaps, and mortgage-backed securities are examples of derivatives.

Call And Put Options

Call options offer the right to purchase, while Put options grant the right to sell. They are also known as European options, which can only be exercised on the date of exercise, and American options, which can be exercised at any time throughout the contract's term.

When the time comes for the buying party to exercise the option, if it does, two situations occur:

Whoever appears as the seller of the option will be obliged to do what such contract indicates; that is, sell or buy the asset to the counterparty, in case he decides to exercise its right to buy or sell.

Who appears as the option buyer will have the right to buy or sell the asset? However, if it doesn't suit him, he can refrain from making the transaction.

An option contract usually contains the following specifications:

• Exercise date: the expiration date of the right included in the option.

• Exercise price: agreed price for the purchase/sale of the asset referred to in the contract (called an underlying asset).

• Option premium or price: amount paid to the counterparty to acquire the right to buy or sell.

• Rights acquired with the purchase of an option: they can be Call (right of purchase) and Put (right of sale).

• Types of Option: there may be Europeans, which are only exercised on the date of exercise or American, to be used at any time during the contract. There are, besides, other more complex types of options, the so-called "Exotic Options."

In international financial markets, the types of options that are traded on organized exchanges are typically American and European.

Why Uses the Options?

Option operators must understand the complexity that surrounds them. The knowledge of the operation of the options allows operators to make the right decisions and offers them more options when executing a transaction.

Indicators:

• The value of an option consists of several elements that go hand in hand with the "Greeks"

• The price of the guaranteed value

• Expiration

• Implied volatility

• The actual exercise prices

• Dividends

• Interest rates

The "Greeks" provide valuable information on risk management and help rebalance the portfolios to achieve the desired exposure (e.g., delta coverage). Each Greek measures the reaction of the portfolios to small changes in an underlying factor, which allows the individual risks to be examined:

• The delta is a measurement of how quickly an option's value changes in response to changes in the underlying asset's price.

• The gamma measures the rate of change in the delta with the changes suffered by the price of the underlying asset.

• Lambda, or elasticity, is a method of determining leverage, often known as "indebtedness," by comparing the percentage change in the value of an option to the percentage change in the price of the underlying asset.

• Theta calculates the sensitivity of the option value over time, a factor known as "temporary wear."

• Vega measures the susceptibility of the option of volatility. Vega measures the value of the option based on the volatility of the underlying asset.

• Rho evaluates the value of an option based on the risk-free interest rate and indicates the sensitivity of the option's value to interest rate fluctuations.

Therefore, the Greeks are reasonably simple to determine if the Black Scholes model (considered the standard option valuation model) is used and is very useful for intraday and derivatives traders. Delta, theta, and Vega are useful tools to measure time, price, and volatility. The value of the option is directly affected by maturity and volatility if:

• For a long period before expiration, the value of the purchase and sale option tends to rise. The opposite situation would occur if, for a short period before expiration, the value of the purchase and sale options is prone to a fall.

• If the volatility increases, so will the value of the purchase and sale options, while if the volatility decreases, the value of the purchase and sale options decreases.

• The price of the guaranteed value causes a different effect on the value of the purchase options than on that of the sale options.

- Usually, as the price of the securities increases, so do the current purchase options that correspond to it, increasing its value while the sale options lose value?

- If the price of the value falls, the opposite happens, and the current purchase options usually experience a drop in value while the value of the sale options increases.

Options Trading Basics

An option is a contract in which the buyer has the right, but not the duty, to purchase (call) or sell (put) a particular amount of an underlying asset at a specific price on or before a specific date.

If you own an option, your potential profit is unlimited and limited to your investment. If you buy an option, your potential profit is capped at the maximum value of the underlying asset minus what you paid for it.

Option Pricing Method

Stocks are purchased, and the investor sells call options on the same stock which they have purchased. The number of stock shares you have purchased should match the number of call options you have sold.

The investor purchase put options to gain equal shares after buying the stock shares. Married acts as an insurance policy in contrast to immediate losses call options with a particular strike price. At the same time, you will sell similar call options at a higher strike price.

An investor purchases an option with cash from outside while simultaneously works an out of the cash call choice for a similar stock.

At the same time, the investor purchases both a call and a put option. The two alternatives ought to have a similar strike cost and expiry date.

The investor purchases the call option out of cash and the put choice simultaneously. They have a similar termination date; however, their strike cost is extraordinary. The expense of the information strike ought to be not exactly the expense of the call strike.

Feature of the Options

Option contracts include typical terms and conditions for exchange-traded options. The following four elements for any exchange-traded option are specified in each contract option:

Underlying Security

Only a limited number of company shares referred to as the underlying securities, offer options traded on the ASX. The exchange determines these underlying securities based on their own set of guidelines. There is no control over the exchange-traded options issued with their shares by the companies themselves.

Contract Size

On the ASX, all contracts for exchange-traded options have a standard contract size of 100. Before that year, for all exchange-traded options contracts in Australia, the standard contract size was 1,000 shares. It aligns the ASX with the US markets, where the standard contract size is 100 shares per contract offer.

Expiration Date

Every option has a limited life depending on the expiry date of the option. The expiry date is the last day the contract can be exchanged (bought or sold), and all untrained options expire.

American style options can be exercised before the expiry date at any time. The bulk of options traded on the ASX are called in the American style. Nevertheless, there is another design type called choices for European style. It is only possible to practice European style choices on the expiry date and not before.

The expiry date of stock options is Thursday before the month's last Friday. Therefore, the expiry date is quoted as a month instead of a specific date. Options will be cited as having expiry dates set on the March, June, September, and December financial quarters, plus monthly expiry dates for the next three to six months, depending on the options category.

Strike Price

If the option is exercised, the exercise price, also known as the strike price, is the price at which the remaining shares can be acquired or sold.

It determines the strike pricing for all options posted on the ASX options exchange.

There are various strike prices for each expiry date option for each underlying security.

New strike orders will be issued as the market value of the underlying security rises.

Premium

The premium alternative is the only part that the exchange does not standardize. The premium is the amount at which a buyer and seller buy and sells the contract.

The price of buying and selling shares on the stock exchange is dictated by the supply and demand powers. Buyers put in offers to buy the stock, and sellers put in bids to sell their stock, which decides the market price when they touch. For alternatives, this is not the case.

Option premiums are calculated by a mix of factors, including the underlying security's market value, the option's strike price, and the expiry period.

Option premiums (or prices) are quoted as "cents per share" overstocks. You need to subtract the "cents per share" by the number of shares protected by the option (usually 100) to determine the overall premium for a particular option. Therefore, a $1.50 swap traded offer will cost you $150.00 to purchase ($1.50 per share or 100 shares per contract). With the trading and exchange fees, you would also have your transaction fees on top of that.

Type of Trading Options

There is a wide range of types and styles of options accessible. This segment gives a picture of each kind just as some essential wording each option investors should be comfortable with.

Call Options

A call option gives the investor the right (not the commitment) to buy the fundamental stock, security, item, or other instruments, at a particular cost within the contract's time. The predefined cost is known as the strike cost. A speculator who is bullish on the stock, which means they anticipate that the stock should go up within a short time or inside the particular period, would buy a call option.

For instance, say Investor A thinks stock XYZ will post high income one month from now, and the stock will go higher. So, they buy a call option on the stock for $20. The option agreement determines that they can buy 100 portions of XYZ at a strike cost of $100 within the following sixty days. If the cost of the stock falls beneath $100, then they won't practice the option. The agreement will terminate uselessly, and they will have lost the $20 price tag. In any case, if the cost of the stock transcends $100, state to $130, then they will practice the option, buy the stock for $100, and afterward, sell it at the higher market cost. They have now made a pleasant benefit.

Put Options

A put option is something contrary to a call option. It gives the owner the right (however, not the commitment) to sell the fundamental stock at a predetermined value (the strike cost) inside the predefined period.

An investor who is bearish on the stock, which means they think the stock cost is going down, would buy a put option.

For instance, say Investor B thinks stock XYZ is overrated and will decrease in cost throughout the following sixty days. Then they buy a put option on the stock for $20. The agreement gives them the option to sell the stock for $120 within the following sixty days. If the stock transcends $120 per share, then they would not practice the option. It would lapse useless, and they have lost their underlying speculation. If rather the cost of the stock dips under $120, to state $90, then they would practice their entitlement to sell the offers at $120 and pocket the distinction as a profit.

Make A Profit Using Call and Put Options

There are various ways you can use call and put options. For instance, assume you believe that portions of US banks selling for $200 per share are undervalued and will go higher in the following couple of months. You need more money to buy at least 100 portions of stock, yet you might, in any case, want to bring in money from the ascent in the stock. For this situation, you could buy a call option on the stock, which would cost just a small amount of the stock's cost. So, you buy the call option, and you presently reserve the option to buy 100 portions of the stock at $200 whenever in the following sixty days.

You may be thinking about buying the stock in the next sixty days for $200 per share if I don't have the money; the appropriate response is that you don't need to buy the stock to make a profit. If your impulses are right and the stock cost rises above $200, then your call option will turn out to be increasingly important. At the end of the day, as the stock value rises, the value of your option agreement likewise rises. You will have the option to sell the option agreement itself, rather than the stock,

30

and make a benefit. The higher the value rises, the more your agreement will be worth.

This works a similar route for a put option, but you need the stock cost to fall in this situation. As the cost of the hidden security drops, the value of your put option will rise. The further the value falls, the more important is your option.

As should be obvious, by buying options, you can profit whether or not the stock is going up or down in cost.

Styles of Options

The past segments have reviewed the two essential sorts of options, calls, and puts. This segment will assist you in understanding the different styles of options accessible.

Most options you will buy will be categorized as one of two classifications: American or European. These are once in a while known as vanilla options. The principle distinction between the two is the point at which you can practice the option.

• American options: American options can be practiced whenever before the expiry date. Most options on stocks and value are of this sort. These are additionally the kind of agreements exchanged on fates trades.

• European options: European options must be practiced on the lapse date characterized in the agreement. These sorts of options are, for the most part, exchanged over the counter (OTC) advertisements.

The two options styles' values are determined marginally distinctively, and their termination dates are also unique. American options lapse the third Saturday of the month, while European options terminate the Friday before the third Saturday of the month.

Similitudes between the two incorporate the result and the strike cost. The result, either for calls or puts, is determined similarly for the two kinds. In like manner, the strike costs ordinarily are the equivalent.

Extraordinary Options

While the over two styles are the primary ones most investors will manage, there is an assortment of increasingly colorful option sorts to know about too:

• Bermuda options: Bermuda options are in the middle of American and European options. In this kind of option, you are permitted to practice them on numerous dates during the agreement time frame.

• Barrier options: Barrier options are not the same as the different sorts talked about so far in that all together for the option to result in the cost of the basic security must cross a specific level. They can be either be put or call options. There are four sorts of barrier options, which are plot beneath:

o Down-and-out: A Down-and-out barrier option gives the holder the privilege, however, not the commitment to buy (on account of a call) or sell (on account of a put) portions of a hidden resource at a foreordained strike cost since the cost of that advantage didn't go beneath a foreordained barrier during the option lifetime. That is, when the cost of the hidden resource falls underneath the barrier, the option is "took out" and no longer conveys any worth. Hence, the name out for the count.

o Down-and-in: A down-and-in option is something contrary to a done for barrier option. Down-and-in options possibly convey value if the fundamental resource's cost falls beneath the barrier during the

32

option's lifetime. If the barrier is crossed, the holder of the down-and-in option has the option to buy (if it is a call) or sell (if it is a put) portions of the hidden resource at the foreordained strike cost on the termination date.

o   Up-and-out: An up-and-out barrier option is like a done for barrier option, the main contrast being the arrangement of the barrier. Instead of being taken out by falling beneath the barrier cost, up-and-out options are taken out if the cost of the hidden resource transcends the foreordained barrier.

o   Up-and-in: An up-and-in barrier option is like a down-and-in option; anyway, the barrier is set over the present cost of the hidden resource, and the option might be substantial if the cost of the basic resource arrives at the barrier before lapse.

•   Basket options: A basket option, otherwise called a rainbow option, is an agreement wherein the worth depends on at least two basic resources. The option to practice the option is reliant on the costs of every fundamental resource.

•   Capped style options: In this kind of agreement, the most extreme benefit is set up. Capped options contain an arrangement where the option is practiced consequently if the fundamental security arrives at a specific set up cost. These kinds of options offer the author of the option a most extreme sum that can be lost.

•   Compound options: These are fundamental options to buy an option. Additionally, it is called split-expense options because the holder must compensate two premiums, one forthright and one if the option is worked out.

• Lookback options: This style of option supplies the holder of the option to either buy or sell the fundamental security at its top (on account of calls) or most reduced (on account of puts) cost over a predetermined period.

• Asian options: Asian options, otherwise called normal options, depend upon the mean (normal) cost of the fundamental security over a particular period.

• Binary options: Binary options have a payout that is either a fixed sum or nothing by any stretch of the imagination. There are two sorts: money or-nothing and resource or-nothing. The holder will get a fixed measure of money in the primary kind if the option lapses in-the-money. In the advantage or-nothing assortment, the holder would get the value of the hidden security. Otherwise called digital options, win big or bust options and fixed bring options back. The bit of leeway to this kind of option is that the potential return is a known sureness before the option is bought. Notwithstanding, once bought, they can't be sold before the lapse.

• Forward start options: Forward beginning options start with a vague strike value that will be resolved later on.

• LEAPS: LEAPS represents Long-Term Equity Anticipation Securities. LEAPS are equivalent to customary options except the more drawn-out lapse dates. A LEAP can have a lapse date that is as long as three years away. The favorable position to this kind of option is there is much more opportunity for the basic stock, and along these lines option, to move toward the path you need it to.

• Index options: Notwithstanding buying options on singular protections, you can likewise buy options on a stock list. These can be engaging even though they give an introduction to a whole gathering of stocks. List options are adaptable and can fit both moderate and theoretical investors' systems during both a bull and a bear showcase. Most file options are European style options.

Pricing

Pricing in Trading Option is when the price of a stock, index, future, or other financial asset is determined by a market. The most common type of pricing in trading option is by using a "bid-and-ask" spread. If the bid and ask prices are identical then they said to be at parity and it indicates that there is no price pressure on either side. The most basic pricing in trading option is based on the spread between the bid and ask price. In this case, the best price to buy something is the lower of the bid and ask. If a stock trades at a premium then it's possible that there is a crowd on one side or another of your trade

If you're not sure how to choose which kind of trading options for you, an experienced, professional trader can help you make a decision that makes sense for your situation. This article will give you some information about pricing in trading option, but only basic information.

Here are the tools to use for pricing in trading option:

Bid Price: The price at which an individual is willing to buy your option Trade.

Ask Price: the amount that an individual is willing to pay you, or sell you, your option trade.

Price of Asset: The current price range of your asset. This may be the stock price, index prices, future prices, etc. For example, if you are trading stocks then this would be the "ask" or "bid" price of the stock (depending on whether you're buying or selling shares). If you're trading options on futures, then this would be the current futures price (also known as the futures quote). The price of the asset may also be the lowest price (or best price) to buy your particular option.

Bid-Ask Spread: The difference between the bid and ask prices. This is usually the value of a spread. The bidding price is what you need to find out in order to place an order to buy. The asking price is what you need to find out in order to place an order to sell. There's not much activity at these prices, but that doesn't mean it's a good time to take any trade. Sometimes retail traders may trade at rates below parity and still do very well for themselves by taking advantage of arbitrage opportunities provided by pricing in trading option.

Benefits of Options Trading

There are a few of the primary benefits of trading in options and why you may consider purchasing or offering options as a part of your total trading method. We will also learn the significant dangers in buying and providing options, remembering that the risks included in options are substantially different for buyers of options than the risks for sellers of options.

When purchasing options, you invest in an asset with no real worth, which may be worthless within a few months. As you will quickly find, there are numerous benefits of trading options that can be used in a wide variety of methods.

We will now describe a few of the main advantages of options. These are extended attributes that apply to options. As we talk about the types of options in more detail and the methods used for each kind of option, you will see the benefits (and drawbacks) of trading options.

A benefit to a seller will typically equate to a downside to the buyer and vice versa. The factor this operates in the marketplace is, the reason or strategy used by the seller is different from the idea the purchaser has participated in the agreement.

When evaluating the benefits of using options, you likewise need to think about the risks associated with your particular options method.

Speculation

The capability to trade online and the listing of options on the ASX make it very simple to purchase and offer options. The options trading makes it possible for traders to buy an option contract with the intent of selling the options before the expiration date for a revenue. The traders may have expectations of an increase in the option (due to a change in the underlying security cost). And no objective of ever exercising the option if your option has intrinsic value. The value of your options will change much in line with the change in worth of the underlying stock. You will also see a fall in quality that is unrelated to any change in worth of the hidden security but is due to a fall in the option's time value as it nears expiry.

How options move with changes in the value of the underlying stock. These movements are for options that have an intrinsic worth in their premium.

As a speculator, you can acquire call options if you expect the underlying security rate to increase. As the security rate's underlying price rises, your options' intrinsic value will increase by a similar amount if you anticipate the underlying security rate to fall. Your method may be to buy put options as the price of the underlying security drops. The intrinsic options' value will increase by a similar amount. To produce a profit, you need the worth of the underlying security to move in your favor before the expiry date, and you would need to offer your option on or before the expiration date.

When purchasing and after offering American style stock options to generate short-term revenue, you need to ensure you sell your options before the expiry date. This requires the cost of the underlying stock to move in your favor before the expiry date.

Idea

When speculating using options, you need to represent the fall in time worth of your option and your ideal costs when assessing your trading opportunity.

Diversification

The use of options can offer you the opportunity to benefit from the motion in a stock rate at a portion of the stock price. This permits you to construct a varied portfolio for a lower preliminary expense. This comes at a cost as your options include a value for the time of expiry, which will decrease to no over the option's life.

Income Generation

When selling an option, you get an advance premium from the purchaser of your option. The premium kept, whether or not the option has worked out. This premium can produce an income stream if carefully selected options are sold on a systematic basis. The seller maintains the premium and has no further commitment if the options are not exercised.

There are several methods based on offering options to generate premium income. The goal is to sell options that are not likely to be worked out or purchase back (closeout) your options before the expiration date if there is a danger they will be exercised.

Disadvantages Of Options Trading

Before you start trading in options, it is important to be aware of the disadvantages which this type of trading offers.

Understanding Technical Analytics

This is the examination and exploration of market activity through the study of charts and graphs. The data pulled from these charts can give analysts guidance on future price movement.

Tax

Although a lot of online platforms provide a facility to make a tax-free trade, you should bear in mind that the entire capital gain amount is taxable. This will be a burden for you if you have a longer-term plan while having a low tax slab rate. In this case, you should bear in mind that the tax slab rate is effective from 1 April 2019. You should also check the tax rate schedule available from the Income Tax Department.

Commissions

As with any other stock, you will need to pay commission charges for making a trade. However, as these trades are done online, the charges are usually much higher as compared to traditional investments. Instead of those direct charges, those online trading outlets charge a much higher fee as the spread, due to the risks involved in trading options.

Time Value Decay

This risk is closely related to the charges which are levied for making trades. Options are not traded with cash value. Instead, they are traded by purchasing the 'option' to buy or sell the stocks at any point of time during the duration of the contract. There are two types of options contracts. The first is the Call option which gives an investor the right to buy the stocks at the option price set by the contract. The second is the Put option which gives an investor the right to sell the stocks at the option price set by the contract.

Loss Of Investment

Options trading can get risky even if there is no uncertainty of gains, due to time value decay. Trading in options involves added risk. This risk refers to the fact that the option holder might lose some or all of the initial investment, due to the time value decay. Time value is calculated by finding out about the value of their option at the trading deadline.

Lower Liquidity

As with any other form of trading, liquidity is a crucial factor to consider in options trading. If a trade is in a highly volatile stock or in a stock with a high rate of turnover, a trader might not be able to get stocks at a reasonable price. In addition to this, if a trader is unable to get stocks that have been sought, they have no option other than to keep their position open or take a loss. In such a case, if a stock shows the volatility in one direction, the option price will rise.

Complicated

Options are complex, and there are many technical factors that are involved when trading options. This is especially true when trading options in volatile stocks or in highly manipulated stocks.

Tips For Getting Started on Options Trading

Although it seems complex and can include a wide range of strategic approaches, it's relatively easy to start trading options.

You need a broker, and you will need to compare fees and account minimums so that you can choose one that is affordable and meets your investment style.

From there, it's time to develop your strategy for trading options. Like most investment options, trading strategies is dependent on your personal goals and tolerance for risk and can range from simple to complex.

Create A Brokerage Account

If you're interested in trading options, you'll need to open a brokerage to access your transactions—this can be done online or through a standard broker account. Be sure you fully grasp what's involved in creating a brokerage account before you do that.

Compare the options trading commissions between different brokerages. Some firms do not even offer commissions on trading options.

Carry out some research online and read the reviews of brokerage firms that are on your shortlist. Get knowledge from the mistakes of other people so you won't have to repeat them.

Observe for scam trading platforms and sites. Always thoroughly research the platform before you deposit any money. Avoid any platform with negative reviews or possible fraud reported.

A cash account will only permit the purchase of options to create a position. If you desire to sell an option to set up an account without the underlying asset, you will need a margin account.

If you want to trade online, make sure that your online brokerage accepts secure payment forms, like a secure credit card payment gateway or a third-party payment service such as PayPal, Payoneer, Skrill, Bitcoin, etc.

Get Approval to Trade Options

You will need approval from your brokerage before you start buying and selling options. Brokerage firms handling an account set limits based on experience and money in the account, and every firm has its own criteria to ensure that the customer knows what they are doing. You can't write a covered call without an options account. Brokerage firms want to make sure before trading that customer have a full understanding of the risks.

Covered call writing means selling the right to purchase your stock at a strike price during the option duration. The buyer has the right to do so, not the seller. The stock must be in the brokerage account and cannot be sold or exchanged while the call is pending.

Start with "Paper Trading"

Resist every temptation to risk hard-earned money with a technique you've just learned.

Instead, go for paper trading or practice. Make use of a spreadsheet or a practice trading software to enter "pretend" trades. Then review your returns for at least a few months. If you make a decent return, work your way to real trading slowly.

Paper trading is different from real trading, as there is no mental pressure or commissions involved. It's a good idea to learn mechanics, but it's not a predictor of actual results. Real options trading is a very high risk, which can result in substantial losses for the investor. You can only trade with money you are willing to lose.

Join A Forum of Traders of Like Minds Online

If you're experimenting with advanced trading options strategies, you'll discover that a vital source of information (and help, after a few tough losses) is an online trading platform. Locate a forum to enable you to learn from the successes and other failures.

Think Of Other Strategies for Trading Options

After you have made some successful trades, you can get cleared for more advanced options trading strategies. However, start trading on paper as well. This will make it much simpler for you to carry them out in real trading.

One such strategy is the "straddle," which includes trading on both sides of the market, purchasing a put and a call option with the same strike price and date of maturation so that you restrict your exposure. This strategy is most successful when the market moves up and down rather than in a single direction. There is also a risk that only one side will be exercisable.

A related strategy is the "strip." The strip is like a straddle but is actually a "bearish" strategy with twice the downward price movement's earning power. It is comparable to the straddle in its implementation, but with twice as many options purchased on the downside (put options).

Know More About the Greeks

Once you've perfected simple options trading and choose to move on to more advanced options trading, you will have to learn about the Greeks. These are measuring that traders use to maximize their returns.

Practical Example

We will talk about essential trading habits and give you examples of excellent option trading strategies. Remember this information can be used to decide to take part in any trading.

The medium and long-term investment is ideal for those who want to build capital or diversify and enhance savings over time naturally and at reduced costs. Given their versatility, ETFs can be used in different medium and long-term investment strategies. They can support or replace traditional instruments, thus allowing them to achieve the set objective. Currently, the range of ETFs is so diverse that any FCI can be replicated (at a much higher cost)

A strategy to invest its capital in the medium to long term is to resort to investment funds, whose popularity has grown progressively over the last twenty years. One of the funds' main characteristics is allowing the underwriter to enter the market with modest capital and obtain professional management that will allow them to obtain positive results over time, with moderate risk. Investment funds should favor more active management, even if this does not always happen.

In addition to weighing on their final return, they are the highest management costs to which the same funds are subject. Their impact is felt particularly in times of slowdown or stagnation of the market. In light of this situation, the investor could find it convenient to substitute the investment in funds with that of ETFs that aim to follow the evolution of its benchmark index carefully while offering the maximum possible transparency.

In advance, it cannot be said whether it is better to invest in funds or ETF; to make this choice, you have to decide if you want the manager to move away from the benchmark (and from which benchmark): this possibility is called "active risk." Active risk is not necessarily bad because some managers are better than others. Still, in reality, they are few, and, not always, you can find them. If you decide to move away from the underlying risk, you must be convinced that:

- Good managers exist.

- That they can do better than their benchmark.

- Above all, be able to find them.

If you think you can complete each of the three phases, it is appropriate to rely on active funds. Otherwise, ETFs are preferred because they cost less and carry precisely where you decided to go without additional surprises.

The techniques for choosing the ETF that best suits your investment strategies are different; an interesting methodology is applied to sector rotation. The market is made up of different equity sectors, corresponding to the different economic sectors and their continuous alternation from the origin to the expansion and contraction phases. Thus, the moments in which all the economic sectors grow or decrease simultaneously are quite rare. The concept of sector rotation is useful to identify, on the one hand, the stage of maturity of the current primary trend and, on the other, to select those sectors that have a growing relative strength. For example, sectors sensitive to changes in interest rates tend to anticipate both the minimums and the maximums.

The sectors sensitive to the demand for capital goods or raw materials generally tend to follow the market's overall trend with delay. Through ETFs, it is possible to immediately position on a specific stock without necessarily being forced to buy the different securities belonging to that particular basket. It will be possible to obtain immediate exposure to this sector, benefiting from its value growth, besides the advantages linked to the diversification.

It is also possible to invest using relative strength, investing, perhaps, on a stock exchange index while benefiting from its growth in value and the advantages linked to diversification.

For example, if one thinks that the US market should grow in relative terms at a given moment to a greater extent than the French one, it will be appropriate to make the first one and underweight the second one. This decision can be reached by analyzing the relative comparative strength between the two markets, which compares two dimensions (composed of market, sector, securities, or other indices) to show how these values are performing comparably. Respect for each other. The trend changes expressed by relative strength generally tend to anticipate the actual ones of the financial activity to which it refers. Therefore, it is possible to use the relative strength to direct purchases towards ETFs that show a growing relative force.

ETFs' high flexibility also allows the construction of guaranteed capital investment; in times of financial turbulence, investors often turn to products that provide capital protection: those provided by financial intermediaries often have high charges for customers. It is possible to build a guaranteed capital product by yourself, which respects your personal investment needs. The central point of the logic of guaranteed capital is interest rates and the duration of the investment. At the base of all, there are central concepts of finance: the higher the interest rates, the greater the return on the money as the duration increases, you earn more because money "works" longer.

In many years, the money we will obtain can be brought to today, as for bills that follow the discount law (the technical term of bringing the future money to today). You can quickly answer the question: "to have 100$ in seven years, knowing that the rates are at 5%, how much money do I have to invest?" This statement indicates how much money is needed to invest today to get the desired amount at maturity. The bonds that allow only the fruits to maturity, without paying interest during their life, are called zero-coupon bonds (zcb) and are quite common on the market. If for example, I want to have $100 at maturity and interest rates are at 5% I will have to invest in zero-coupon bonds $95.24 (if the deadline is between one year) $78.35 (if the deadline is in five years) $61.39 (if the deadline is ten years) €48.1 (if the deadline is between fifty years) and $23.21 (if the deadline is thirty years)

In effect, by building investment with guaranteed capital, one only has to decide how to invest the remaining part of the initial $100 that have not been allocated in the zero coupons. An ideal solution could be to invest in options because they can amplify any yield thanks to the leverage effect. If you have a less aggressive investment profile, ETFs are excellent tools to build guaranteed capital investment. If, for example, we assume a ten-year investment with rates of 2.5% for that maturity, the portion to be invested in zcb is equal to 78.12%. In comparison, the remaining 21.88% will be invested in the ETF.

This investment strategy achieves a minimum (not real) "money" return target with few operations, as the zcb provides for the repayment only on the nominal amount of the loan (not discounted to the inflation rate). Therefore, it is a valid methodology for those who intend to make investments with clear objectives and have little time to devote to monitoring the values as only an operation until expiry may be necessary. Unlike a guaranteed capital product offered by any financial intermediary, an investment of this kind built independently with ETFs can be dismantled entirely or in pieces (selling only the zcb or existing assets, ETF) to meet any need.

Naturally, only at maturity will there be a certainty of the pre-established return and, throughout the loan, a temporary adverse trend in financial variables, (rates rise by lowering the zcb and at the same time decreasing the value of the ETF) could result in the liquidation of losing positions. The same consequence would be selling a structured bond, with the advantage that "doing it at home," the commissions are much lower. You can separate the two components and, if necessary, liquidate only one, according to specific needs.

The Profitability of Equity (ROE)

This is the ratio between the net result and a given company's net assets. Mainly from equity investments is an essential parameter as profitability higher than the cost of capital is an index of an enterprise's ability to create value. Therefore, it should guarantee a higher capacity for the securities' growth in the phases of the rise of the market and resistance in the reflexive phases. From this point of view, the Roe is always held in strong consideration by those who choose to invest in shares today.

Dividend Yield

This is the percentage ratio between the last distributed dividend and the share price. In particular, it measures the company's remuneration to shareholders in the last year in the form of liquidity. This parameter is often taken into account to identify the securities to invest in since a company that can distribute dividends is generally a good company.

In this case, as with all the other selection parameters, it is necessary for a broader and more complete analysis since a high level of this indicator could also mean that the company has made few investments or has little prospect of growth. For this reason, looking at the dividend yield as a primary factor in determining the securities to invest in the options market is reductive. The dividend yield only makes sense if accompanied by considerations of the listed company's business plans and industrial plans.

Common Options Trading Mistakes

Nobody can claim to be a flawless trader. We all make mistakes, even the best of us. When we note our mistakes and admit to them, we get a chance to become better. Some mistakes are often repeated over and over again, yet they can be avoided. There are, however, some general mistakes that you need to avoid if you are to trade options successfully:

Trade Without an Exit Plan

As a trader, you must learn to regulate your emotions. This is true whether you are trading in stocks or options. You always need to have a plan, work with the plan, and stick to it no matter your feelings. An exit plan is necessary whether you are losing or winning. In short, have an upside exit point and a downside exit point.

Trading With a Fixed Mind

Many traders often trade with a fixed mind, thinking they are always right. Sometimes, even when evidence is available to the contrary, traders still stick to their positions. Instead of insisting on being right, the focus should be on being profitable, and this means being flexible and having an open mind.

Purchasing Out of The Money Options

Some of the cheapest options in the options market are the out-of-money options. Many beginners often rush to buy these because of their low cost, and this might seem like, therefore, to them. However, there is a reason these options are so cheap. Most of them have very little chance of ending up in-the-money, so that they may be worth nothing eventually.

If you are to purchase these options, you have to be accurate in terms of time and direction. You will still lose out even if the direction is accurate if you sit on them too long. The expiration date is often the most crucial determinant about whether the options will finish in-the-money.

To fix this, try and go for straight long puts and calls. Get these in-the-money options as soon as possible. While they are likely to be more expensive, they possess a better chance of success and will likely earn you a profit.

Fundamental Analysis

To make the best trades, you have to gather as much data as possible regardless of what market you are working in. There are two ways to get the most out of any of the data you gather, the first is via technical analysis, and the second is via fundamental analysis.

Fundamental analysis looks at specific factors based on the underlying asset for the market that you are working in.

Fundamental analysis is typically considered easier to master than concepts less expressly related to understanding market movement exclusively.

Before You Enter a Trade

You have to know a few things before you enter the market to understand how to filter out and consistently pick good trades.

Portfolio Balance

Before you do anything, you need to look at your portfolio balance first. When you're planning a new trade, it's always important to ask yourself why you need that trade and how it will affect your portfolio. Do you even really need it? For instance, if your portfolio already has plenty of bearish trades, it would generally be better for you to avoid adding more.

You need to reduce your risk in every situation, so the key here is to balance out your trades. That's how one develops a great portfolio, risk diversification. When you have many bearish trades in hand, look for bullish trades to offset the risk and vice versa. Once you internalize this, it becomes far easier to focus on your portfolio needs and filter out the rest from the first moment you start looking for a new trade.

Liquidity

Liquidity is straight-up one of the essential qualities of a good, tradable option. You don't want to remain with an illiquid option, no matter how lucrative it looks. Here's a simple rule to follow when looking for a new trade: for it to be a good trade, the underlying stock should be trading at least 100,000 shares daily. If the numbers are less than that, the trade isn't worth your time.

In a market as big and efficient as the one we have, the calculations only become more accurate over time. Similarly, when considering the underlying options, there should be a minimum of 1,000 open interest contracts for the strikes you are trading for it to be a good trade. It ensures quick entry into and exit from the market. Remember, liquidity is important.

Implied Volatility Percentile

When a trade satisfies the two criteria, it's time to move on to the next step—the IV percentile. You need to check how high or low the implied volatility of an option is, which is measured by using percentile scores. Let me explain with an example:

Say, if AAPL has IV of 35% but IV percentile of 70%, it means that while the current volatility is low, in the last year, it was higher than what it currently is (35%) for more than 70% of the time. So, the implied volatility for AAPL is relatively high, and you should be looking to employ premium-selling strategies.

Picking a Strategy

Picking a great strategy is as much a matter of eliminating as it is a matter of selecting, perhaps even more so. You can easily eliminate many strategies once you have a good idea of the IV and the IV percentile of the underlying stock and how it affects the options. For example, it's easy to eliminate strategies like debit spreads and long single options when you know the IV is high and the pricing rich. Then it's time to consider our risk tolerance and account size to pick the best strategy out of the ones left (iron condors, credit spreads, strangles, etc.).

Strikes and Month

Your trading style and goals also play a big part in how you decide to pick trades. Some people are more risk-averse than others, and that's okay. You should always select the right strategy based on the risk level you're comfortable with. If you're selling credit spreads, let's say, and you have the option to sell them at either a strike price that has a 90% chance of success of a strike price that has a 65% chance of success, you need to decide which option you want to go with based on the level of aggression you're comfortable with. It needs to fit your trading style and your goals.

You also need to do is give yourself sufficient time. This makes sure the trade can work out. This means that you should place low IV strategies at sixty–ninety days out and high IV strategies at thirty–sixty days out. You should read up on Theta value (one of the Greeks) and how it affects volatility.

Position Size

It is one of those areas where even some of the more experienced traders fail. You must understand this concept so you can make great trades often. Before placing a trade, you should always carefully assess your position size. As your trading position gets bigger, so does the risk, but this isn't linear, as many studies have shown. The risk increases exponentially, and one bad trade could easily lead to a blown account in this case. I strongly advise you to start with small positions as a beginner and continue to do so even when you're an intermediate. Your risk scale should be a sliding scale of 1–5% of your total balance on which all your trades need to be placed.

The cash or margin you use to cover a trade is what we call risk. For example, when selling a $1 wide credit put spread for 50 cents, you would need to cover it up with a $50 margin. You use this $50 margin to base your trade-off for each trade you make. If your account is worth $20,000 and you wish to allocate 3% of your account (it fits the 1–5% sliding scale criteria), you can take $600 of risk (3% of $20,000). You divide this by $50, and you get 12, which is the number of spreads you should sell at most. If this number is a fraction, always round down and never up.

Future Moves

You must've heard the popular saying that a chess grandmaster can foresee as many as 20 moves ahead. A good options trader also plans and foresees future moves. You're going to lose to the market more often than not if you're not thinking a few moves ahead. Always have another plan in case things go nasty and you need to shield yourself from losses. And while shielding yourself from a losing trade is important, it's also important to plan how to turn a loss into a winning one.

Sometimes, you won't be able to make a winning trade. That's just how the market works; some trades go wrong no matter how well you plan. But you need to keep asking yourself important questions constantly. When you do this, your mind stays sharp and ready to jump into action to formulate a new plan or make an adjustment as and when the need arises.

Choosing A Broker

When engaging in day trading for a start, one of the most crucial decisions you are going to make is picking. This will determine the types of securities you can trade (for example, many brokers aren't going to work with cryptocurrencies for trading), how much you pay for each of your trades, and what kind of platform you use. Picking out a competent and experienced broker, who is easy to deal with, can make a great deal of difference in the results you achieve with your trades.

When working with a broker, and having determined that they trade in the securities you are interested in, becomes their compensation plan. You want to know if it is going to be profitable for you and your trading pattern. Since day trading requires various minor transactions during the day, you don't want to have a compensation plan where the broker gets an already fixed payment every time you make a trade transaction.

There are varieties of different payment patterns that your broker can select, and you need to understand and accept the one you find most reasonable. Going with a fixed payment for the entire year would be nice, but you can also choose the payment pattern where your broker receives a particular commission from your earnings, so if you don't earn anything on a trade, you won't be running at a loss. Whichever broker you decide to go with, though, make sure to let them know the payment pattern you would like to operate with them from the start.

One of the prerequisites you must consider when selecting a broker's company must include:

Margin and Account Necessities

Let's go through the criteria for the accounts and the margin range among brokerages. Many investment companies may need initial minimum investments of $2,000, and others will need minimums of $10,000.

Margin criteria for stock options transactions depend on the trading company. The criteria for the investment margin can often differ as a result of the type of options approach that you want to use. For beginners, certain broker companies would ask you to sign a document showing your trading prowess in options.

Having completed the program, grasping extensively the methods that you plan to use, and have effectively traded paper, you will comfortably say that you are an expert in trading options. You can sell and acquire shorter and longer calls/puts while provided with margin rights. The contract that you sign is insurance for the trading company to be sure that margin-protected individuals grasp all the implications of the transactions they position. For example, in bullish economic conditions, an upcoming trader who sells naked calls might quickly hit a snag. If you were conversant with this course, you would be much less likely to position these trades because the potential risks are endless. Among the advantages of sharing trading, you will still be aware of the overall costs and potential earnings.

In case you are not buoyant enough to meet the requirements of your chosen brokerage company for maximum margin rights, you will still be able to purchase long calls and puts. Brokerage companies would usually require more money or better trading opportunities for short-selling calls and puts. If you find yourself in this situation, just divert the long calls and puts them into constructing your fund before you can organize a maximum margin-protected stock options account or find another brokerage company.

What Are Stocks

Stock is seldom called shares or equity. That is a sort of defense indicating an extent of control as it affects the company that issues it. When an individual has stocks, he/she have the right to a portion of the company's earnings and assets. One can acquire shares and trade them at stock markets, but it doesn't imply that there are no other places to trade and acquire stocks. In private sales, too, stocks may be exchanged. In the business sector, there is hardly any investor that does not have shares in their portfolio. They will be in accordance with rules that regulate and protect consumers against depraved procedures until transactions can be treated as legal. Markets have exceeded them when compared with other financial products.

Option Trading Platform

A vital aspect of options trading is the platform that one uses to trade. This is because options trading requires monitoring and requires a continuous analysis of trends. Performance is also monitored, and since the trade is impacted upon by a complex of factors, one must choose a suitable platform for trading.

A good platform should offer a lot of opportunities for traders. These are opportunities to orient beginners into trading, development for the existing ones, and actualization for those with a record on the platform. Such a platform should also prescribe the available products and any resources that subscribers on the platform can benefit from to push themselves to profitability.

With the technology developing at high speed, platforms continue to improve by the day. This is both complicating the trading itself as well as providing avenues of spreading awareness about the business. A platform should have the ability to offer the best possible experience for the traders to do trade and grow both in experience and returns without meeting a lot of platform limitations and frustrations.

A Platform Takes Trading to the Holders

Trading involves a lot of complexities that may sometimes be scary. It makes people lose interest as soon as they develop it. They perceive it as too complicated. The impression is that it is a venture meant for the people who have higher comprehension of concepts in the economics specialty and that those who do not a background in this area will have difficulty getting on board.

A trading platform needs to present options trading as a venture that is possible and in which anyone with interest can succeed. The days when options trading and any other forms of trading were presented as a show of sophistication are long gone. In this era, every sector of investment is portrayed as conceivable, and businesses are now being made easier to create a better chance for people to dare. A platform that limits investment so much and is exclusive in terms of how it carries out its trading activities is irrelevant to modern economic patterns.

Platforms, thus, have to be interactive and user-friendly. They should have the ability to encourage users to feel like they can handle the trade. It should also have the capability to gauge the level of use and give feedback about how well they can use it. If it's a website, for instance, it should report the numbers as people visit it and how many eventually end up creating accounts and trading. Counting traffic is essential for feedback that can lead to the creation of a better experience for the users.

Competition

In choosing a platform sometimes, one would want to take advantage of the advantages of different platforms. This is looking at one's style of trading and how they wish to monitor their business and see if a platform is more transparent in handling the tares or whether it offers a clear lens of controlling purchases and sales of options. This is the reason why the various platforms must be assessed in terms of their potential. Usually, platforms are related to the tools of trading. Some of the tools of trading can be found right on the platform of trading.

When a platform of trading also has various tools of aiding trading, it ensures that one can gain a lot of benefits in one place. This makes the platform a utility where a person can visit for more purposes than just trading. It also makes it better. For instance, if a platform has videos that offer trading tutorials. This can make it resourceful in imparting competency in participating in the very sector that the platform operates.

To best benefit from competition, one should understand the type of trade they want to do. This is by naming their price and gauging which platform can serve better in ensuring returns and value generation. This is to avoid going into trading in desperation, and one has to be patient to see if the platform can also come out and meet a trader at their point of ability and also help in trading in comfort where risk is at a minimum.

Types of Trading Platforms

There are various platforms in options trading that one could consider. There is web-based trading that utilizes the power of the search engines. This platform has many operators since the building of websites in the modern age is easy. This is responsible for the growth in the popularity of options trading. People can trade with anyone, open brokerage accounts, make deposits, and participate in the buying and selling of assets in the comfort of their homes.

With the presence of a lot of technological gadgets such as smartphones, tablets, and computers, web-based trading has been easy and within reach. Websites can be built with additional resources for learning and tools that can be an advantage for both novice and seasoned traders. On the websites, regular updates on the market can be posted to keep traders informed about trends, patterns, and even help in analyzing price movements for the subscribers.

The web is also a good platform when it comes to filtering opportunities and options based on suitability and preferences given the various abilities of users. They can be designed to be customizable even when the options markets are standardized.

User Friendliness

Friendliness is also in terms of the efforts that are made to create peer assistance. This is through creating groups of traders that influence each other and can learn from the vast experiences in the trading of the options. This can be a positive influence on the journey to gaining competence and help support an environment where people can relate and interact as they pursue their various financial goals.

Tools to Learn

Upon mastering the various basics of trading and making the initial moves to start trading, one will use various tools that help indicate the advancers and decliners on the market. Greeks are metrics that those involved in options trading capital to ensure maximization of returns. These "Greeks" include the delta matrix that measures the correlation between price movements of the underlying asset relative to the price of the option. The tools for monitoring the movements for these parameters of trading are vital as everyone trades with a focus on minimizing losses while geared towards profit maximization.

Some salient features of options are measured in terms called the Greeks and labeled with Greek letters. It's really essential to understand the Greeks if you're going to get serious about trading options.

•   Beta: Beta is a characteristic of the underlying stock and measures the historical volatility of that stock. It gives equal weight to volatility on the upside as well as on the downside. When you're evaluating a stock, you can get a sense of how variable the stock's price is by looking at the Beta. A stable stock that moves with the market will have a beta value of about 1. If beta is less than 1, it tends to lag the market that is a $1 movement in the market a stock with a beta less than 1 means it will increase or decrease less than $1. Conversely, a stock with a beta greater than 1 means the stock price will move more than the market, up or down. Stocks with low betas are more stable than those with a higher beta. Examples of low beta are utilities. Stocks with a high beta include industries like biotechnology.

• Vega: Vega is a measure of the volatility of the option price. The option price is related to the underlying stock price, but the option price is also variable. Vega is a measure of that volatility, but it's an implied volatility, not a historical volatility as is beta. Vega is the only Greek trading term without a Greek letter symbol.

• Delta: Delta measures the change in the price of an option in response to a change in the price of the underlying stock. For example, if an option has a Delta of 0.45, when the underlying stock changes by $1, the option will change by $0.45.

• Gamma: Gamma measures the rate of change in the underlying stock, not the change itself. Gamma expresses how fast the option responds to changes in Delta. Gamma is expressed as a positive or negative number. A positive gamma indicates that changes in the delta will be correlated with positive movements in the underlying stock. A negative gamma has the opposite indication.

• Theta: Theta measures how much value the option will lose as days pass until expiration comes. The loss is due primarily to the time value of money. As a wasting asset, an option's value will decline because of the concept behind time value. A dollar today is worth more than a dollar next week. This time decay is difficult to calculate and most economic models are complex and often not particularly accurate.

Professional Level Platforms

There is a level in trading where one attains sophistication and attains the intuition to thrive in options trading regardless of the ways market forces seem to behave. At this level, someone needs tools that enable them to edge into the horizon of complexity in trading. The platforms for this professional level exist, and they have to offer tools that are an edge above the basic level. These tools have to offer strategies of competing to control the stocks and rise above the market forces. At this level, one becomes daring, and the possibilities that the platform offers should only be dared by those who have mastered trading and are sure of beating odds as they speculate about squeezing out value-form trades that otherwise be perceived as highly risky.

Mobile Trading

Mobile trading also comes to keep people abreast. This is because opportunities sometimes appear and disappear on people because they aren't using a device that enables them to be precise and timely in decision making and action.

With mobile trading, apps have been developed, some with notification capability. One can customize the apps to ensure that no opportunity comes that is not taken advantage of. Opportunities in trading must be seized and relying on a platform that is less reliable and useful means that opportunities for trading are lost.

What Are We Looking for in Platforms and Tools?

First is the opportunity to learn. There is no worse platform of trading than that which targets only to admit traders who do not understand what they are getting into. The education that a platform has to offer should be free as trading is itself risky enough to prohibit any extra expenses in the process. Platform operators should understand that anyone to visit their platform is a potential subscriber, and they should freely offer support to educate them for the acquisition of requisite knowledge on options trading.

Excellent broker services try to suit customer needs. They ask options traders on their platform what their preferred means of communication is. Whether a live chat or phone call suits the customer or not. They also dedicate a desk for trading communications and queries and have the discipline to listen to customers and their issues with patience. They, in fact, have feedback on the quality of customer service that those who reach out get.

Software Trading Platforms

These are more complex than web-based ones. This is because they are run on the trader's computer, and the trader is required to understand what the software does and interpret it. Even when the brokerage can assist, software-based platforms require the trader to have enough technical know-how to read charts, graphs, and understand patterns that represent various components of options trading.

For beginners, a complex platform is to be avoided by all means. This is because one is bound to engage in aspects of trading that they do not understand. A trading platform needs to be clear and simple. The interface should not be too busy as to scare away those traders who aren't accustomed. This is the reason why operators usually separate the platforms that as designed for basic use, which is suitable for novices, and advanced trading for the seasoned ones.

Then a broker has to offer a tutorial that guides the user on how to navigate their platform. Everything should be explained, even those that one would deem to be obvious. Screenshots can even be available to be categorical and emphatic. This ensures that a broker has offered all possible assists for the trader to benefit from the offers and products on the platform successfully.

Cost Implication

The trader needs to know that some brokers may have charges attached to some of the services, resources, and tools that they provide on their platform. These must be assessed in terms of their worth and whether the costs are necessary. Making some tolls premium may be an indicator of quality but not always. This is particularly the case when other platforms provide similar services toll-free.

Screening tools are particularly the ones that are bound to attract charges because they have abilities to analyze and assess market trends. They can think about the trader and help him in decision-making. One should read about the specifications of the tools and ascertain what they or cannot do. This is so they know if they are customizable according to the needs and conveniences of traders.

Some charges can even be attached to the quotes update feed. Usually, the quotes can be accessed in real-time for those who want to see them in real-time. The quotes are useful in influencing idea generation and sometimes can tip people of opportunities in the market. There is usually a delay for those who access the quotes updates for free.

Include The Procedures for Trading in Demo Accounts of Leading Online Brokers.

The use of shares, whether it is to collect dividends or to speculate on their listing, is an increasingly widespread and interesting practice. The risk of loss is always present but depending on the way you buy and sell your shares; this risk can be reduced. If you are wondering how to buy and sell the shares of large, listed companies online, here are some explanations that may interest you.

Buy shares to become shareholders

A large part of private individuals and institutions that buy stocks do so to become shareholders.

It is the simplest use of actions and their main purpose.

In fact, when a company issues its shares, it is possible to buy them directly online.

However, for the already listed shares to do so, it is necessary to go through an intermediary, which can be an online broker or an online bank.

Buy and Sell Shares with Online Banks

The easiest way to buy and sell shares is to go through one of the placement products offered by banks and, in particular, by online banks. Thanks to the 100% online operation of these banks, you can easily pass your purchase and sale orders directly via the internet without moving.

The advantages of this system are numerous because it is your bank that will take care of executing your orders and then buying and selling your shares. To take advantage of stock market shares through these systems, you must underwrite an Investment Plan in Shares, a securities account, or life insurance, which are the main banking products on the stock market. The only drawback of this method concerns the expenses that may be higher than those that you would have to pay if you bought and sold the shares yourself.

However, bank commissions rarely exceed 4%.

One of the main advantages of bank placement products is that market intermediaries supervise your purchases and sales of shares and you can benefit from advice.

Buy and sell shares with online brokers

Another method is to contact an online mediator. Their operation is almost identical to that of online banks, with the difference that you do not enjoy assistance and advice, but at the same time, the costs are lower because you decide for yourself what actions to buy or sell.

These online brokers also allow trading through stock market shares, without actually having to buy them. To do this, you just need to speculate on the evolution of their value. The tools that allow you to proceed in this way are CFDs.

Ultimately there are several methods to buy and sell shares on the internet. Before deciding on one or other of these solutions, take care to correctly evaluate the commissions involved as well as your level of knowledge on the stock exchange. Depending on these criteria, each of these two methods has different advantages. It is also good to understand the quotation system of an action to be able to speculate on this type of asset.

Choosing and using a financially sound and responsive brokerage should be a high priority for every trader. And that brokerage should provide access to every trading venue: equities, options, futures, or forex. Many brokerages are running slick TV ads that do not qualify. When you examine the list of financial products served by brokerages, you may be disappointed. Some well-known brokerages support stocks and options. But they do not offer futures or foreign exchange. So, walk away and keep looking.

Many who are new to trading select a brokerage because they know someone who has an account with that particular brokerage. But this is not how you should choose your brokerage, particularly if you are an entry-level trader. Conduct some research before you make a final decision. You want to choose a brokerage that fits your investment and trading style. This may not be the same as your friend's.

Fortunately, you can use the Internet to evaluate brokerages. A website provided by the Financial Industry Regulatory Authority (FINRA) provides a substantial amount of information about the conduct of both individuals and firms. Of course, it essentially lists regulatory citations, and never makes recommendations or posts complimentary comments. The listed regulatory citations are mostly for failures in oversight or careless trading practices. Corresponding fines are also listed. You can read these to find FINRA citations similar to the following:

This permits you to see a list of former employers, the time a counselor has been working with financial securities, and any past FINRA citations that may exist.

Charts like these never tell the entire story. And like so much Internet content, they are often misleading. The range of securities supported in addition to the sophistication of the trading platforms was ignored. The Kiplinger rankings are far from accurate when you consider the breadth of services, platform technologies, number of branch offices, availability and quality of customer support, and more.

In the author's opinion, TD Ameritrade's thinkorswim platform would rank #1 for trading options and stocks. It has the most extensive feature set. And Trade Station, which is superior to many of those listed, wasn't even included. Furthermore, a trade that costs $0.0050/share looks good at first glance. But a 4,000-share trade costs $20 in commissions. Most experienced investors know brokerages will likely reduce their commissions and exchange fees to meet competition. This is especially true for high-net-worth clients and/or high-volume active traders.

Full-Service and Discount Brokers

Full-service brokers typically provide financial investment counselors. The counselors may suggest financial securities products, managed funds, or recommend investment management companies with which they maintain business relationships. These full-service brokerages also provide research and education to their clients. The fees charged by full-service brokers are usually higher than those charged by discount brokers. Required minimum account deposits may also be higher than those required at discount brokerages. Besides, the maintenance of a minimum account balance may be required.

Discount brokerages also require a minimum account deposit and the maintenance of a minimum account balance. This can range from $500 to $1,000. And experienced active traders who manage their own trading activity have little interest in receiving trading advice from an investment counselor, who may not have as much trading experience or knowledge as their clients.

Many old-timers have clear recollections of their dealings with the traditional brick and mortar brokerage houses and the so-called "stockbrokers" in their employ. They'd look at the lists of stocks in the daily news or the Wall Street Journal. When they spotted a trade opportunity, they'd phone their broker to put on a trade, and pay a $70 commission. They also remember receiving phone calls from their broker who had been advised by the "boys in New York" to solicit their clients to buy shares of stock that were part of an issue that their brokerage house was promoting. Some clients wised up and referred to these stocks as the "stock de jour."

This was an unscrupulous "pump and dump" practice used by brokerages to increase the sales of an underlying stock held within the brokerage's own portfolio. Once the solicitations drove the price up as a result of the sudden influx of buy orders, the brokerage dumped the stock for a profit, leaving their clients "holding the bag." Obviously, they couldn't do this every day, and it didn't take long for regulatory agencies and clients alike to catch on. But according to many, this actually happened. Today, the regulatory agencies watch for these kinds of practices and levy heavy fines when detected.

But stories like these often drive traders to the discount brokerages. All an experienced trader wants or needs for that matter is access to the market through a full-featured, reliable trading platform, reasonable commissions and exchange fees, and fast execution times.

Develop a checklist that evaluates prospective brokerages. Look for the following, arranged in no particular order:

•   Account types (Brokerage, IRA Rollovers, checking, bill pay, savings, money market, etc.)

•   Minimum balance requirement.

•   Transaction fees.

•   Margin interest rate.

•   Supported trading venues (equities, options, futures, and/or forex)

•   Execution speed.

- Access to different trading venues.

- Trading platforms (online for PCs and/or Macintosh Computers)

- Trade scanning engine(s).

- Market research (either web-based or trading platform-based)

- Account access via brokerage website.

- Trading via brokerage website.

- Earnings and dividend releases.

- Mobile trading apps (iPhone, Android, iPad, Android Tablets, Windows Mobile)

- Paper (simulated) trading for practice.

- Back trades (testing strategies with historical pricing data)

- Support (online chat, telephone, e-mail, and text messaging)

- Training (live and/or online)

- Complete financial reporting (monthly, year-to-date, prior years, 1099s, IRA minimum required distribution calculations, commissions paid, margin fees, etc.)

- Nearby branch offices.

Financial Security and Stability

When opening an account, you may want to know who is underwriting the security of your account in addition to the maximum amount protected. Congressional action in 1970 requires all brokerages to register with the Securities Investor Protection Corporation (SIPC). The

SIPC is to brokerages what the FDIC is to banks. The SIPC protects the brokerage accounts of each customer. If the brokerage firm is closed due to bankruptcy or fraud, the SIPC protects customer assets up to $500,000 in securities and $100,000 in cash. If your accounts exceed these insured values, you may want to consider distributing your funds across more than one brokerage, although very few investors actually do this.

Although the SIPC protects against bankruptcy and fraud, it doesn't protect against market losses caused by a decline in security values. If a brokerage firm does fail, the SIPC works to merge the failed brokerage into a successful one. Failing this, the SIPC will transfer a client's securities to another firm. If stocks or bonds are missing from an investor's portfolio, the SIPC will rebuild portfolios by replacing every missing share of stock or bond, penny for penny, up to the insured limits.

Many investors never consider what can happen to their account holdings in the event of a run on the financial markets or an institution. What effect can this have on the stability of your broker, also called broker-dealer?

It's somewhat reassuring to know that during such condition's insurance is extended and liquidity facilities are created to back depositor accounts. The Securities and Exchange Commission (SEC) has instituted several reforms on liquidity. These liquidity reforms ensure that each broker-dealer maintains a suitable reserve to cope with inordinate levels of client withdrawals.

Despite these regulations, short-term unstable funding can prevent broker-dealers from order fulfillment. This can be due to a short-term lack of funds required to carry temporary imbalances in the volume of buy and sell orders. This impairs the ability of traders to buy and sell a wide variety of stocks and bonds. It can also have the effect of bringing trading to an abrupt halt.

Many investor-traders remember the failures of broker-dealers Lehman Brothers and Bear-Sterns during the housing mortgage fiasco of 2008. As a result of the lessons learned then, many broker-dealers have increased their capital holdings, increased liquidity, and reduced their holdings in risky assets. All of these policies are attempts to protect themselves against the reoccurrence of events like those that brought down these huge brokerage houses.

As the holder of a brokerage account, you should know that the potential for broker-dealer failures still exists. Both broker-dealers and banks have been encouraged to form either asset-rich bank holding companies or intermediate holding companies to help spread capital risk.

Broker-dealers typically find short-term security by negotiating repurchase agreements with underwriters, such as money market funds. This provides the financing needed by broker-dealers to fund their transactions. In exchange, the underwriters receive reasonably low financing fees. The money market funds, among a few others, avoid long-term, risky securities. They happily settle for shorter-term, low-risk securities with less vulnerability to a potential market run.

Passive Income

Passive Income is an act of trading time for money. It's an act that many people say they would do if only they had the time to allocate to it, but few actually ever do it. When odd jobs are offered or there is no work available at your day job, you can afford the luxury of choosing not to work for money. Perhaps it is because you can't trust yourself with no income, or perhaps it's because you know that working too hard would leave you exhausted and unable to achieve anything else. Whatever the reason, there are plenty of ways to 'work for your money'.

Passive Income is not always easy to achieve. It takes time, dedication and discipline. It typically requires that you work only when you want to, in your spare time away from family or work commitments. You must also be prepared to take risks and invest some of your savings into a business which often seems risky at first glance. However, taking on these risks can result in a massive boost in passive income — allowing you to afford the luxuries that money can buy, while giving you a more fulfilling lifestyle.

Active Trading Vs Passive Trading

Various people often ask about stock trading as being a source of passive income or not. The active nature of traders will be investing a great amount of effort and time in turning a profit. Well, their activity of the trade will be taken as the primary form of focus.

In the case of passive income, the earnings are derived from a limited partnership, rental property, or by using other enterprises, in short, anything in which any individual is not involved actively. Passive income is generally taxable. So, suppose you are looking out for generating passive income by using options. In that case, you must hand over the capital to a broker whom you trust, any automated system, or by investing your capital through copy trading.

Passive Income Pros and Cons

Right before we start with the various techniques of earning passive income by using options, it is very important to first learn about the benefits of passive income and its drawbacks. An obvious benefit related to passive income is the limited amount of time you will have to commit. But this also indicates the extreme pressure on the decisions of investments that you are going to make. Passive trading might sometimes end up in a very slow profit stream when you compare it with active trading. There are also certain dangers that you are most likely to oversee while monitoring your income. Ultimately, this might result in losing a great amount of potential profit.

Techniques For Generating Passive Income

There are some ways in which passive income can be made:

Automation

To make the whole game of passive income a lot easier, some people often opt for automation. When used properly, the automated systems can make you capable of generating substantial nature of profits. This is because there is only a specific trade number that one can make in a day. A unique algorithm can easily enter and exit the positions as soon as the pre-determined criteria have been met.

They will also permit you to trade in several markets at one time. Right after you have successfully programmed your criteria, passive income can also be generated while sleeping. Some of you might doubt the capabilities and efficiency of this system. But, around 75% of the trades made on New York and NASDAQ's stock exchange originate from all these algorithms and define their efficacies.

Software

Right before you start having passive income by using automated trading, you must lookout for the perfect software. Try doing your research, and never forget to check the assessments first before you start investing. Once done with your research, and you have chosen your software, you must develop a great strategy. You can start by creating a small checklist for your parameters of trading. You can easily consider these:

• When to enter positions and when to exit them.

• Size of the position.

• Trading timeframe.

• Stop losses and targets.

Back testing

Before starting any automated system for generating passive income from options, you will need to back test the strategy first. This will permit you to test the entire system right before you risk in your capital. You need to run the software you chose right against any historical price data to gauge how efficiently it performs. You can easily identify the issues, if there are any, and fix them before investing.

Copy Trading

Another great way of developing passive income is by the method of copy trading. In place of giving in all your energy and time for developing the strategy and monitoring all the tasks, you can easily benefit by following the experienced traders' success. You need to select a trader, and a program will then be mimicking the trader's buying and selling by using your capital. But it might happen that the traders will take a minimal percentage of the profit that you make. But it also comes along with certain drawbacks:

• Risking your capital: You need to be always prepared because of the market volatility. You might also lose the entire capital you have invested in. If you are risk-averse and if you cannot see yourself with huge losses, it is better not to opt for this option.

• Choosing a trader: Picking a trader might turn out to be a challenge. Any aggressive nature of options trader can clear you out within several days. Always consider the instrument of approach and choice that they use. You are also required to check the updated history of the trade of the trader. All you are looking out for is a consistent and steady form of results.

• Not keeping up with the trades proportionally: Certain sites might not permit you to trade proportionally. But, for good, the traders, most of the time, invest only in particular quantities. So, you need to ensure that you only focus on copying the trader.

Using Put-Selling Strategy

It is often regarded as the most efficient way of developing passive income. The best strategy that can be used is by buying stocks when they are overvalued instead of being undervalued. As you sell puts that are overvalued, you can rake in huge premiums from the buyers. You can also determine the option value based on the implied volatility of the same. Implied volatility can help in measuring the amount of greed and fear that is priced into any option. When the implied volatility is considerably high, the prices of the options will tend to be overvalued. This can easily attract many investors.

The stocks that are your own will be trading much above the strike price for the duration of the option's lifespan. This indicates that you will be collecting the option's premium, and you are not required to purchase any of the underlying stocks. While this is taken as an ideal scenario, there are other scenarios for you to understand.

When the underlying stocks fall under the right level in the middle of the strike price and strike price that is less than the option's premium is the second scenario. The investor will be winning as the adjusted cost basis is better than the one currently present in the market, right after considering the received premium of the option.

The third scenario is when the stock price goes below a point below the strike price, subtracting the option's premium. This is often taken as the worst-case scenario for any trader of cash-secured put.

How You Can Make Money by Selling Puts?

Selling puts will be allowing you to set the stock strike price according to you at which you want to buy it. Selling puts is much more attractive than selling covered calls as you are not required to post your capital, which is beneficial for purchasing the shares. You need to follow certain steps right before selling the puts:

- Finding out a stock that you would like to buy.

- Deciding the entry price that you want to buy the shares.

- Evaluating the implied volatility.

- Setting the risk parameters.

81

Technical Indicators

A technical indicator is a computer-generated index of market sentiment associated with a particular asset or market. They are often used by traders to predict the direction of the market and find profitable opportunities. Technical indicators can be grouped into three categories: trend following, oscillators, and cycle analysis.

Lagging Indicators

Lagging indicators are indicators that closely monitor and follow a stock's price pattern. This is why they are called lagging. These indicators are solely based on the last data. They are hence excellent at indicating any trend developing in the market or if a stock has entered a trading range. Lagging indicators can, for instance, point to a stock with a major downward trend and will most probably continue falling.

Future Trends and Pullbacks

Keep in mind that lagging indicators are not recommended when it comes to predicting future pullbacks or rallies. These indicators can indicate the trends that have developed until the latest point. However, they cannot point to future trends or events, even just for the following couple of days. Some common lagging indicators popularly used by options traders include ADX indicators, the Moving Average, and the MACD.

Therefore, lagging indicators are excellent at pointing at the developing trends but are poor at predicting or forecasting future stock price movement.

Leading Indicators

The other very useful technical indicators are the leading indicators. These technical indicators are beneficial at predicting future events. They often provide relevant information regarding possible crashes and future price gains. Some of the leading indicators include momentum indicators. These are capable of predicting or gauging the momentum of the price movements of a stock.

Momentum indicators are more like tossing a football in the air. No matter how high the ball rises, we know that it will eventually fall back to the ground. We may not know when it will stop going up, but we are sure that it will do so at one point. This is the genesis of momentum indicators.

Leading indicators such as the momentum indicators are excellent at revealing if a stock price has gone too far down or too high up. They also let us know whether there is a reduction in the momentum of the price movement. When the price moves too high, it simply means there has been an over-purchase of the stock. In such cases, then, the stock has been overbought.

Should the price move too low, then this says an oversupply of the stock, and buyers are possibly dropping it. If the stock has been overbought or oversold, it will not remain in this state for long. We can, therefore, make a deduction that a pullback is likely to happen. Most momentum indicators and the RSI are good examples of leading indicators.

Lagging And Leading Indicators

Most traders appreciate both lagging and leading indicators because they are both invaluable. You are informed of any possible price pullbacks and slowdowns as a trader. Ideally, you should never rely on just one of these indicators but both. This way, your predictions, and trades will always be accurate and reliable.

Most indicators sometimes produce false signals occasionally. Since this is a risk that you want to avoid, we recommend using at least two or three different indicators. Identify 3 specific indicators that you like, and if they all give you positive information about a stock, you can feel confident enough to invest in it. There are essentially hundreds of different indicators in use across the world. Most seasoned traders will have developed their technical indicators to predict the markets accurately. You should learn how to use about 5 different technical indicators. This way, you will have a wide variety of options to choose from.

Top Technical Indicators

We have noted above that there are hundreds of different technical indicators currently in use. However, some are absolutely crucial for options traders. If you can learn how to use about 5 of them, you will have a strong foundation for your technical analysis. Here is a look at some of the more important ones:

Average Directional Index Indicator, ADX

The ADX or average directional index is a popular indicator that is mostly used for confirmation purposes. It essentially works to confirm the information or signals that are produced by other indicators. This technical indicator works by measuring the strength of any given trend. For example, you can use the ADX to measure if an upward trend or maybe even a downward trend is slowing down or gaining momentum.

This average directional index, ADX, combines the positive directional indicator, +DI, and the negative directional indicator, -DI. The -DI or negative directional indicator tracks the downward trend, while the +DI or positive directional tracks the upward trend in the stock market. When these two indicators are combined together, we get the Average Directional Index. This combination of two strong indicators produces one powerful and unified trend strength indicator.

The +DI is showcased as a green line in the chart above, while the –DI is shown as a red line. The ADX indicator itself is shown as a fat black line. We note that there was a strong stock trend from late February until mid-April, as indicated by the ADX. The stock was trending upwards.

It is possible to notice that the ADX indicator never went below the 20 marks. This is a clear indicator of when the stock ever traded flat. An accurate assessment is mostly visible from the stock price. In general, we notice that this is an accurate assessment as it is visible from the strike price. There was a remarkable uptrend for the first three months and the last three months indicate a downward trend.

Oscillating Indicator

The ADX technical indicator also happens to be oscillating. Its oscillations range from zero to a hundred, with zero representing flat trades while a hundred represents a plunging or rising stock. Please note that the ADX indicator showcases the strength of a trend only without pointing its direction.

Also, the ADX values often range between 20 and 40. Rarely will you see ADX values above 60. The reason is that high values above 60 points to a trend that usually appears when there is a long recession or a long bull run. Any values that are below 20 often point to a stock entering the trading range.

According to our chart above, we notice that signals produced by the Average Directional Index, or ADX, indicator, any move that is way below 40 points and above will indicate the trend's slowdown. The options strategies always rely on large volumes of shares, so a trend that is slowing down is undesirable. Therefore, as a trader, if you notice any ADX indicator is a simple pointer, the trend is slowing down, and that now would be the best time to buy out.

Similarly, any index indicator that moves above 20 indicates that the sideways trading strategies are over because a new trend is currently developing. It is an indication that the current upward trend is almost drawing to an end. As such, it is time to make a positive movement that can be either bullish or bearish. Also, sometimes the ADX indicator can move way above 20. This is always a clear indication that the current upward trend has started to fade.

Again, in our chart above, the ADX technical indicator produced a signal right in the middle of April. You should learn how to look for stuff and be observant. Signals on this example can be obtained by observing and noting where there is. When the +DI, green, and wring signal process above +61422 –5840364. When the two indicators, the +DI, and the –DI cross paths with each other, we will identify our signal here. When they meet together, they should form a bullish signal. You should, therefore, always base your investment opportunity on recommendations from the map. Experts advise that you make use of only one or additionally two types of indicators. This way, you will be sure of what to do and when to do it.

Bollinger Band Strategies

Another technical strategy that is commonly used to showcase the voracity of stocks is the Bollinger strategy. There will always be an opportunity to learn from the boss. A Bollinger Band strategy or theory is mostly meant to showcase how volatile the stocks are.

This is a simple technical indicator as it is composed of a simple moving average and both its upper and lower bands. These upper and lower bands are only about 2 standard deviations away.

We can confidently say that standard deviation is more like statistical tools. This is because the majority of movement occurs around these positions. When you use the Bollinger Band theory, you will discover that it only works as a guide or gauge and should, therefore, be used in conjunction with other indicators. If you learn how to apply these indicators, then you stand a great chance for success.

The Bollinger Band theory operates optimally in conjunction with the twenty-day SMA or simple moving averages. We also need the standard deviations of the twenty-day SMA to create the Bollinger Bands. Some of the strategies that emanate from this indicator include long-term and short-term Bollinger Bands. The shorter-term bands which are less than twenty days are highly sensitive to price movement while the longer-term bands that exceed twenty days are less sensitive and more conservative.

Better Options Trading

For traders who want to supplement their income, or branch out to options trading, there are a number of courses available about how to do so. Searching for these courses online is preferable over in person because you can find the best one at your convenience and trade in almost any currency.

These beginner courses provide information on types of trades and what each type means for the trader. They also go over different strategies and how their probability and return change depending on changing market conditions. Some beginners might be afraid that they will end up with too much information, but this is not the case; these tutorials pause frequently with questions to answer, giving people time to think about what has been shown them.

There are courses for different languages, so even beginners from other countries can learn from beginner courses to get a good feel of options trading. The cost is not that high, and it is an amazing experience that can greatly improve your life.

How Relevant Is a Trading Network for Options?

The demand for options is very complex. Trading without a framework is like building a house without a plan. Movements of price, time, and stock will all impact your earnings. You must be mindful of each of these variables. Emotion can easily be swayed as the market shifts.

With a program, the response to these natural and usual emotions can be controlled. How much did you sit and watch a trade losing money when your order was filled?

Have you seen a stock price spike when you think of buying it? It is important to have a clear strategy in place to make rational and reasonable trade decisions. You can boost your trade executions by designing and following a good program, as emotionless and automatic as a machine.

Advantages Of Trading Scheme Options

• Leverage: Selling options have the stock market leverage. You can manage hundreds or thousands of shares with options at a fraction of the stock price itself.

A change in stock values from 5–10% may be equivalent to an increase of 100% or more. Seek to focus on percentage gains against dollar losses in your exchange. It needs a radical shift in traditional thinking, but it is necessary to effectively manage the trading system.

• Objectivity: A successful trading scheme of options is focused on observable parameters that allow signals to be bought and sold. It takes the subjectivity of your business so that you can focus on predetermined variables that trigger explosive trade.

• Flexibility: Most options traders can tell you that options give your trading flexibility. The demand for options makes it remarkably easy to take benefit of short-term positions.

You may build strategies for overnight gains with clearly specified risk with earnings events and weekly options. There are ways to benefit from the trend to the range of any market situation.

• Security: The options trading program will serve as a hedge against certain investments, depending on an acceptable strategy in prevailing market conditions. This is a way of using defensive puts.

• Risk: The trading structure of good options reduces the risk in two essential ways. Cost is the first method. The option prices are very small relative to the same quantity of inventory. The second way issues end. A successful system will easily reduce losses and keep them low.

The more tools in your toolbox, the more able you are to adjust business conditions. Unless the markets were to act in the same way every day, trading would become a play for children. To start designing your options trading, you have to build a trading strategy or strategy to lead you in the right direction.

Start with the basic framework and tweak it to identify and enhance your trading criteria. It takes time and experience to develop a productive options trading program that can return 100% or more in consistently profitable businesses. If you are pleased with your machine parameters, you can look at your own program's automatic trading.

Steps To Options Trading System

• Pick a strategy: You can select any strategy to start developing a program. The best way to get going is to buy calls and puts. You will add new approaches to your trade to boost your method by researching and understanding more about how prices move.

Adding long-term equity protected calls and protections is a sensible next step so that you can debit your account by generating a monthly or weekly cash flow.

• Trade: It is time to trade once you have established the fundamentals of your strategy. Start small contracts, one or two contracts, and keep detailed transaction records. Be sure to include the underlying inventory price at the time you purchased or sold your right.

Notes will allow you to evaluate how and where you can change. When you add new trading requirements to your system, your statistics should be strengthened. If not, it is time to re-evaluate your given criteria.

- Measure-assess the successes and shortcomings: The duration of the research depends on the amount you traded. If you trade actively, it is important to have a weekly or monthly summary. Compare your winnings to your losses. Zero on the main factors that make up a good trade and seek to change your parameters to boost your results.

Analyze your mistakes as frustrating as they can be. Tune the requirements to avoid the same errors again. Analyzing your errors is as critical, if not more, to research your productive businesses.

- Change: If there is a losing streak or spot in your options trading scheme, change it. Adjust it. It's no shame to be wrong. This is part of the trading industry. The irony is that you are blind to and repeat your mistakes.

You will keep the device in line with changing business patterns and conditions by identifying the blind spots and making modifications. It sounds so basic, but perseverance and discipline are important.

- Know: A method of trading is not static. Keep your mind engaged by learning always. The more you research the stock market and the trading system of options, the more you learn and the better.

Swing Trading with Options

What Is Swing Trading

Swing trading is a simple trading philosophy, where the idea is to trade "swings" in market prices. There is nothing special about swing trading in a commonsense kind of way because it's a buy-low and sell-high method of trading with stocks. You can also profit from a stock when the price is declining by "shorting" the stock.

So, what distinguishes swing trading from other types of trading and investing? The main important distinction is that swing trading is different from day trading. A day trader will enter their stock position and exit the position on the same trading day. Day traders never hold a position overnight.

Swing traders hold a position at least for a day, which means they will hold their position at a minimum overnight. Then they will wait for an anticipated "swing" in the stock price to exit the position. This time frame can be days to weeks, or out to a few months' maxima.

A swing trader also differs from an investor, since at the most, the swing trader will be getting out of a position in a few months. Investors are in it for the long haul and often put their money in companies they strongly believe in. Alternatively, they are looking to build a "nest egg" for one to three decades or even more.

Swing traders don't particularly care about the companies they buy stock in. They are simply looking to make a short-term profit. Although swing traders may not hope to make instant profits like a day trader, they won't hope for profits from a company's long-term prospects. A swing trader is only interested in changing stock prices. Even the reasons behind the changes in the stock prices may not be important. So, whether it's Apple or some unknown company, if it is in a big swing in stock prices, the swing trader will be interested.

The chart below shows the concept of swing trading. If you are betting on falling prices, you can earn a profit following the chart's red line. If you are betting on increasing prices, you will follow the upward trending blue line. A bet on falling prices is often referred to as short, while a bet on rising prices means you are long on the stock. This, of course, is another difference between swing trading and investing; investors don't short stock.

Swing trading can be used in any financial market. In the chart above, we are showing a chart from the Forex (currency exchange) market. The principles are the same, so the specific market we are talking about doesn't matter, so it works with options.

Support and Resistance

An important concept often used by swing traders is spotting support and resistance. Support refers to a local low price of the stock. It's a pricing floor that, for the time being, the stock price is not dropping below. To find support, you just draw straight lines on the stock chart. The share price should touch the support level at least twice to be a valid level of support.

Resistance is a local high price. So, this is a high price level that the stock is not able to break above. Again, expect it to touch the resistance level at least twice, and drop back down before considering a given share price for the resistance level.

As the share price moves in between support and resistance, there are opportunities to buy-low at the support level and then sell-high at the resistance level. And you can do the reverse in the case of shorting the stock.

You can enter your position at the relatively high resistance level, then exit your position at the support level.

Of course, support and resistance will not be valid price levels for all time, and stock will often "break out" of support or resistance. This happens when the share price starts a declining trend and goes below the support level, or if it breaks out above the resistance level in an uptrend. There can be more opportunities to make a profit. But, when a stock price is stuck between support and resistance levels, we say it ranges.

Trade with the Trend

The best thing to happen to a swing trader (or a trader of straight call and put options) is for a stock to enter into a unidirectional trend. So, it could be a trend in upward prices, giving you a chance to make large profits before it starts reversing. Alternatively, of course, trends can head downwards, opening up opportunities for shorting the stock.

Trends can exist in many different time frames. It might only last part of a day, or it could last weeks and even months. Learning to spot trends and take advantage of them, with a sense as to when the trends will come to an end, comes with experience and education. A new options trader can benefit by studying educational materials related to both swing and day trading. Hence, they know what to look for in stock charts to spot not only trends worth getting into, but also how to spot a trend reversal that would eat up your profits.

The chart below of AutoZone stock is a simple example of this concept. It's a dream trade, with prices going steadily up with time. But remember nothing lasts forever.

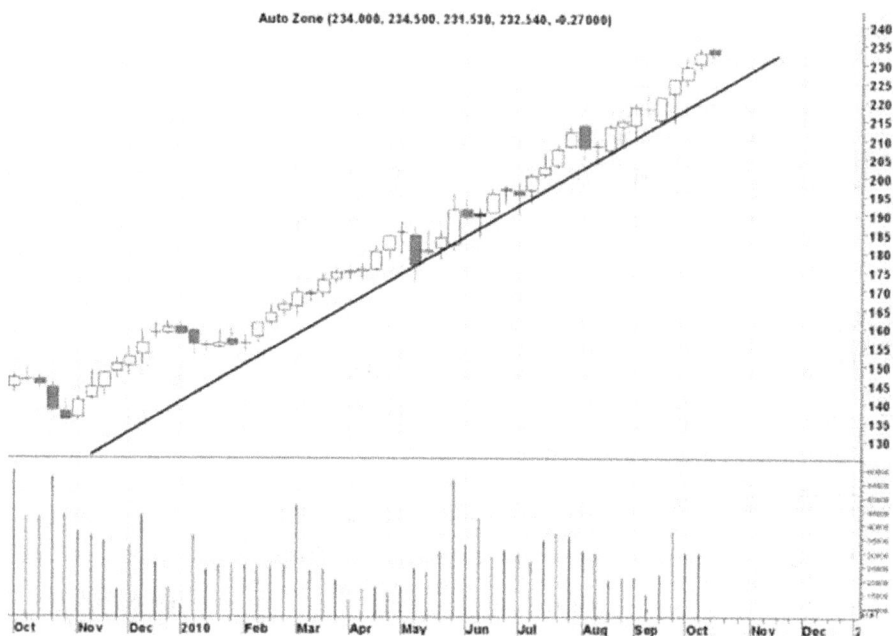

Auto Zone (234.000, 234.500, 231.530, 232.540, -0.27000)

Trading with a trend is something you'll want to look for as an options trader. The time scale of the trend is going to be something important, of course, because you will be concerned about time decay when trading options. Time decay is a concept that a swing trader does not have to worry about.

So rather than being beholden to specific rules, like saying you will trade options like a day trader or like a swing trader, an options trader has to be flexible. You will need to be ready to take advantage of very short term moves in stock price that only last for a day or less, and you'll also want to be in trades that can last days to weeks or even months.

Swing Trading Options

Since options are time-limited, they are a natural fit for the concept of swing trading. Although many of the advanced strategies attempt to take out the direction of share price movement from the equation, if you are buying single call or put options to make a profit, then you're behaving at least in a qualitative sense like a swing trader.

Since put options gain in value when stock prices are declining, buying put options is like shorting a stock. It's quite a bit more accessible, however. Too short a stock, you'll need a margin account, which allows you to borrow shares from your broker.

Shorting a stock's basic idea is to borrow shares from the broker when the stock price is at a relatively high point and sell them. After this, the trader will wait for the share price to drop. The trader will buy back the shares and return them to the broker when the share price is low enough to make a profit.

Of course, shorting stock using options is far easier. The reason is you never have to buy the stock to make a profit from the declining price. You simply profit from the prices of put options which will increase as the stock price goes down.

Going Long on a Stock

If you believe that the price of a stock will rise, you want to buy call options. So, call options to represent the most straightforward or common-sense way to trade options. When you buy a call option, you are betting on that stock. Another way to say this is that you are bullish on the stock.

A good way to go about trading options is to pick a few companies and limit yourself to trading them. The reason is that you are going to have to be paying attention to the markets, company news, and general financial news for any option that you invest in.

If you spread yourself too thin, you will not be able to stay on top of things and find yourself getting caught up in losing trades. The best approach is to keep your trading limited in scope to know what is going on. That doesn't mean you only trade a single call option; you might trade many of them on the same stock.

There are two ways to go about swing trading options. The first way is to look for ranging stocks that are trapped in between support and resistance. Then you can trade call and put options that move with the swings. So, the idea of this type of trading is very simple. First, you need to study a stock of interest and determine the price levels of support and resistance. Then, when the price drops to the support level, you buy call options. Now hold them until the price goes back up near resistance. It can be a good idea to exit your trades before the price gets to resistance so that you don't end up losing some of your potential profits if the price reverses before you get rid of the options.

Trend trading call options can also be very lucrative. In this case, you are looking for significant news and developments related to the stock or even the economy at large. For example, when a company announces that it had big profits, this can be an opportunity to earn money with call options, as the price will go up by large amounts as people start snapping up the stock. When trading in this fashion, you're going to need to know how to spot trend reversals. The idea is the same when you identify a trend in the making, buy call options, and then ride the trend until you are satisfied with the level of profit and sell the options.

Again, it can't be emphasized too much. You always need to take time to decay into account when trading options. So, remember that with each passing day, your options are going to lose value automatically. Check theta to find out how much value they are going to lose. And as we deliberated before, often, other factors overwhelm time decay in the short term long before the price swings to another course.

Trading Dictionary

The basics of options trading are always easy to understand. However, the trade involves more advanced aspects that need time and patience to learn. It is not surprising that options trading has hundreds of terms and jargon, some of which you may never have heard. We have come up with a comprehensive list of the terms used in the trade as a reference tool that you can use when learning more about options.

A

Actions certificates that represent a small part of the property of a company.

Anticipation—The act of a stock trader predicting the security market future before either buying or selling their stock.

Arbitration—To operate in two or more markets at the same time to take advantage of a temporary positive fluctuation in one compensating losses of another and obtain a profit.

Asking price—An initial price at which the security can be sold by the investor in the security market.

Asset—What is being exchanged on markets, such as stocks, bonds, currencies, or commodities.

Assignment—The process of issuing an option seller or writer with an exercise notice instructing them to sell or buy 100 shares of particular equity at a stipulated amount as the strike value.

At the money—An at the money option is one that has a cost that is equivalent to the value of the equity.

Automatic exercise—The process where options that are in the money are exercised automatically, if still in the money during expiration.

B

Base currency—The first currency in a currency pair, and the other currency that determines the price of a currency pair is called a counterpart. Knowing the base currency is important as determining the value of the currencies (national or real) exchanged when a currency contract is negotiated. The euro is the most used base currency against all others. The British pound is the next in the hierarchy of currencies. The main currency pairs against the British Pound are GBP/USD, GBP/CHF, GBP/JPY, and GBP/CAD. The United States dollar is the next predominant base currency. USD/CAD, USD/JPY, USD/CHF are the normal currency pairs according to the main currencies; the dollar is listed as EUR/USD and GBP/USD.

Bearish market expectation—The value or price of an option will decline over time.

Bearish stock—A form of stock that is anticipated to decrease in value over a specific time by a stock market trader.

Bear market—When the overall prices of a market are on the decrease.

Bear spread—A spread that aims at generating profit from bearish price movements.

Bid—The price at which the market accepts to buy a specific currency pair.

Bid price—The highest price of securities such as stocks in the security market a dealer is willingly prepared to offer in exchange for the securities.

Bid-ask spread—The value obtained by calculating the difference between the ask and bid prices of an option.

Black Scholes pricing model—A model that uses factors such as the value of the underlying security, strike price, time value, and volatility to estimate the price and profits made from options.

Bonds—A kind of loan that investors make to their issuers in exchange for a fixed payment (interest); the issuer under different conditions not only pays the interest but also returns all of what was loaned at the expiration of the term.

Break-even point—The point at expiration where an option strategy returns zero profit and zero loss.

Broker— (Definition 1) The person or organization that processes option contract orders on behalf of traders and investors.

Broker— (Definition 2) The professional who is responsible for either buying or selling securities such as stocks for their clients.

Broker— (Definition 3) The intermediary between the secondary market and investors. Through its infrastructure, people with liquidity surpluses can negotiate securities.

Brokerage—An individual or a firm responsible for arranging transactions of buying and selling securities for the sake of getting commission after the exchange is successful.

Bullish—A market state defined by the possibility of the cost rising in the future.

Bullish stock—A type of stock that is predicted to rise in value over a certain period of time by a stock trader in the security market.

Bull market—A state when the overall market prices are increasing.

Bull spread—A trading spread established to generate profit from bullish stock and market movements.

Buy to close order—An order generated when a trader wants to close an existing call position. This is achieved through purchasing contracts that you earlier sold to other investors.

Buy to open order—An order that you place if you want to enter a new position of purchasing contracts.

C

Cable—A technique used by operators to refer to the British pound sterling in the exchange rate of the British pound/US dollar. The term began to be used because the rate was originally transmitted using a transatlantic cable in the mid-1800s.

Call option—The kind of option that gives a buyer authority to buy 100 shares for given equity at predefined prices and expiration periods.

Carrying cost—The cost incurred when using capital to buy options based on the interest received from borrowed capital.

Cash or spot—A platform or live market price. The value agreement in transactions without completion period but at a certain starting price.

Cash account—A brokerage account where an investor is required to make full payments of the securities they have purchased.

Cash-settled option—An option where profits are given to the holder in cash, not in the form of shares.

Central Bank—The main monetary authority of a nation, controlled by the national government. It is responsible for the issuance of the currency; for establishing monetary policy, interest rates, exchange rate policies, and regulation; and supervision of the private bank's sector. The Federal Reserve is the Central Bank of the United States. Others include The European Central Bank, The Bank of England, and The Bank of Japan.

CFDs—Although its exact definition is "contract for difference" and is a financial derivative, its practical meaning is the possibility of accessing an underlying title with leverage. It sounds a bit complex, but in practical terms, it is very simple. Suppose that you are going to invest in an action that is worth $1,000 and has COP $10,000; this would only allow you to buy 10. If you, did it through a CFD, the broker provides leverage by converting your COP $10,000 into COP $100,000, allowing you to buy 100 shares instead of 10. Of course, that extra leverage is not free, and you must pay interest in accessing the product.

Close—To end a trading position. Also refers to the time of the day when the market stops operating and the final option prices are determined.

Closing order—An order that you raise to end a contract that is already in existence.

Combination order—An order that comprises more than one basic order.

Contingent order—An order that allows you to set customized parameters for entering or exiting options contracts.

Contract range—The highest prices of a single contract minus its lowest prices.

Contract size—The number of share units covered by individual contracts. In options trading, the default size is 100 shares.

Conversion—The process by which assets or liabilities denominated in one currency are exchanged for assets or liabilities denominated in another currency.

Cost of interest financing (cost of carry)—The cost or benefit associated with the continuation of open operations from one day to another, calculated by using the short-term interest rate differential between the two currencies that make up the currency pair.

Coverage strategy—A strategy designed to reduce the risk of investments used to require options, introduce positions, short sales, or futures contracts. Coverage can help to ensure profits. The purpose is to reduce the volatility of a portfolio by reducing the risk of losses.

Covered call—A trading strategy used to make profits from existing contracts when the market is neutral.

Covered put—A trading strategy that works together with short selling to make profits from existing positions. This strategy protects your investment from short-term price increments.

Currency—The unit of exchange of a country issued by its government or Central Bank, whose value is basic to commercialize.

Currency option—A form option that has currency as the equity.

Commission—The money you give to brokers or brokerage companies for their services.

Credit—The money you get in your account for selling an option.

Cross exchange rate—The exchange rate between two currencies. It is called the cross-exchange rate because it is not common in the country where the currency pair is quoted. For example, in the United States, a GBP/CHF price would be considered a cross-rate, while in the United Kingdom or Switzerland, it would be one of the primary pairs of traded currencies.

D

Day trader—A person who purchases or sells securities in the security market within a single day.

Debit—The amount of money you give out when purchasing an option.

Derivative—An instrument that obtains its value from other financial instruments. For example, options and futures.

Devaluation—The decrease in the value of the currency of one country in relation to the currencies of other countries. When a country devalues its currency, imported goods become more expensive, while exports become less expensive abroad and thus more competitive.

Differential (spread)—The difference between the sale and purchase price of a currency. It is used to measure market liquidity. Smaller spreads mean higher liquidity.

Discount broker—A broker that only carries out basic order processing for options traders.

Discount option—An option that sells at a price that is less than the intrinsic value.

Dividend yield—A form of a dividend that is illustrated in the form of a percentage of the present share price.

Dividend payout ratio—The relative amount of the total revenue that a company pays its shareholders.

Dividends—The returns that are paid by a company to an individual who owns shares in it.

Drawdown—The consecutive loss in market operations and its potential impact on the income statement, generally assessed within a possibilities test or statistical analysis of the reliability of an operations system.

E

Early assignment—When a contract seller fulfills the requirements of the contract before its expiration period.

Early exercise—The process of closing contracts before they expire.

Earnings per share—The portion of the profit made by a firm that is allocated to each share that is outstanding in the firm's common stock.

Equity ratio—A ratio that portrays how much of the assets in a firm are being funded by the equity shares.

Entry order—An order executed when a specific price level is reached and/or penetrated. The execution is handled by the negotiating table and is in effect until it is canceled by the client.

Entry stop order—An order executed when the price of the coin breaks a specific level. The customer places the order considering that when the price of the coin breaks the specific level, the price will continue in that direction.

Exchange—An operation that combines cash and installment transactions in the same negotiation.

Exchange trading funds—funds invested for trading in the stock exchange trade.

Exercise—buying or selling an options contract at a specific strike price and time period.

Exercise price—The price of each share at which it is sold or bought at expiration. This is another name for the strike price.

Expiration date—The date when a contract stops existing or expires.

Expiration month—The month in which expiration takes place.

Expire worthlessly—A contract that expires worthless is one that returns no profit at the expiration date.

Extrinsic value—Those aspects of an options pricing that are determined by factors not related to the cost of the equity or security.

F

Fixed exchange rate—The decision of a country to immobilize the value of its currency with respect to the currency of another country, gold (or other product), or a set of currencies. In practice, even fixed exchange rates can fluctuate between high and low bands, which can lead to intervention.

Foreign exchange market—The simultaneous purchase of one currency and the sale of another in an extra stock market.

Forex—A very controversial term since many illegal activities also use this word to explain their profitability. This is not an illegal market, and many of the activities that gave rise to its restriction never invested in Forex. In this market, the different currencies of the planet are negotiated, such as USD (Dollar), EUR (Euro), GBP (Pound Sterling), JPY (Yen), etc.

Fundamental Analysis— (Definition 1) A method of analyzing the intrinsic value of a financial instrument in the stock market and its price value in the future.

Fundamental Analysis— (Definition 2) A discipline that seeks to know and evaluate the true value of a financial instrument based on the causes that influence the composition of the price, that is, its value as a commercial profit or its value based on its expected future performance.

Futures—Another financial derivative that allows investors to reserve a product today, providing only a small percentage of its total value. Since they are standard contracts, delivery dates of the products are agreed upon, where the investor will cancel the remaining percentage of the formerly separated titles and receive them. Although many traders use them for speculation (which makes them extremely risky), they were originally created for hedging or coverage.

G

G7—The seven most industrialized countries in the world: the United States, Germany, Japan, France, the United Kingdom, Canada, and Italy.

G10—The members of the G7 plus Belgium, Holland, and Sweden are an associated group that takes part in the discussions of the International Monetary Fund. Switzerland is sometimes involved.

H

Hedge fund—A non-regulated private investment fund for large investors (investments that start with a minimum of $1 million) specialized in high risks, short-term speculations in bonds, currencies, options of stock, and derivatives.

Hedging— (Definition 1) The process of investment that seeks to minimize the risk of trading tour investments.

Hedging— (Definition 2) Through financial derivatives such as CFDs, futures, options, etc. investors can secure the price of a security by making it totally immune to changes in the market price. Suppose you are an oil company and the market price of crude oil is $100 per barrel. If the price reaches $50, your income is reduced by half, but if you cover your production with a derivative of $100 and the price falls to $50, both you and your counterpart pledged to deliver and receive the production to $100 respectively. Now if the oil reaches $150, you will be paid $100. As you can see, it is a way to keep the price fixed.

Historical volatility—Measures the volatility levels of a stock by studying past price movements over a period of time.

Horizontal spread—Spread created from several contracts that feature the same strike price and different expiration dates.

I

Implied volatility—An estimate of the future volatility levels of underlying security based on current prices, using pricing models.

Index option—A contract on the options market whose underlying asset is not stock but an index.

In the money—A contract whose stock value is more than the current cost in the case of a call position; the opposite is true for a put contract.

Inflation rate—The percentage in the change of either the rise or fall of prices of securities in the stock market.

Inflation—A moment where the prices of securities can either experience a sudden rise or an impromptu fall.

Interbank rates—The rates at which large international banks exchange their currencies with other large international banks.

Interest rate—An amount of interest that is paid after a certain amount of time to a stock trader for the money they have invested in the stock market.

Interest—The amount of money an investor in the stock market receives from the money they invest in the stocks purchased.

Intrinsic value—A contract whose equity value is higher than the strike amount.

Investor—An individual who willingly allocates their capital in the stock market to get profits in return after a certain amount of time.

L

Long—What most people are used to in the market. Buy in the hope that the price will rise after closing the transaction. If you buy at a price X, you will earn money only if the price of the asset increases; this is basically a long one.

Leg—Individual positions that form a contract comprising of several positions.

Leverage— (Definition 1) The process of using options to obtain more payoffs from the options market.

Leverage— (Definition 2) The amount, expressed in multiples, by which the final amount traded exceeds the real amount invested. For investors, leverage means increasing profit in value without increasing investment.

Liquidity—The ability of a market to accept large volume transactions depending on volume and activity in a market. It is the efficiency and effectiveness of prices with which positions can be operated and orders executed. A market with greater liquidity will provide more frequent price quotes as the smallest differential buying/selling.

Limit entry orders—Orders that are executed when the price of a coin reaches (without rubbing) a specific level. The customer places the order assuming that after they have reached the specific level, the price will move in the opposite direction to its prior movements.

Limit order— (Definition 1) An order that allows you to trade options at the specified minimum and maximum strike prices.

Limit order— (Definition 2) An entry limit order for a specific position that is programmed to secure the earnings of a position. An entry limit order programmed in a purchase position is a sales order.

Limit stop order—An order that instructs positions to close when certain prices are attained.

Liquidity—The level of availability of a certain financial instrument. In other words, this is a measure of the level of ease that a certain instrument can be bought or sold without affecting the prices.

Listed option—An option that is listed on the options market.

Long bull—A position to buy large volumes of coins as well as to sell them, so that an appreciation of the value is made if the market price increases.

Long position—A position that is created when you purchase a call or put contract.

Lost stop orders—An entry order related to a specific position to stop the position, thus avoiding incurring additional losses. A loss stop order located in a buying position is a stop entry order to sell such position. A loss stop order remains in effect until the position is liquidated or canceled by the customer.

M

Margin—Customers must deposit funds as collateral to cover any potential loss due to adverse price movements.

Margin account—A type of brokerage account where an investor has the choice to get cash from customers for them to purchase securities or other financial instruments.

Margin call coverage—A request for additional funds or other guarantees, from a broker or negotiator, to increase the margin to a necessary level that guarantees execution in a position that has moved against the client.

Margin requirement—This is the amount of money that a trader deposits in their brokerage account to cover for naked option positions. These act as collateral for the brokerage firm to purchase or sell options on behalf of the trader.

Market bubble—A situation where prices of stocks are escalated above their actual value by traders.

Market indicators—Formulas and ratios that can illustrate the gains and losses in the indexes and stocks.

Market order— (Definition 1) An order used to buy or sell a contract at current market prices.

Market order— (Definition 2) An order to buy or sell at the live price of the base currency.

Market stop order—The order that closes a position when certain market prices are attained.

Market size and liquidity—The 10 most active traders' accounts provide the market with bid (buy) and ask (sell) prices. The bid (buy)/ask (sell) offer is the difference between the price at which a bank or a market manufacturer will sell ("ask" or "offer") and the price at which a market manufacturer will buy ("offer") to a wholesale customer.

These offers may not apply to retail customers in banks, who will routinely mark up the difference to 1.2100/1.2300 for transfers, or 1.2000/1.2400 for banknotes or travelers' checks.

Point prices in market manufacturers vary, but in EUR/USD, even in times of high volatility, they are generally not more than 5 pip wide (i.e., 0.0005). This difference, known as "spread," also depends on the brokerage in which it operates.

Recently, some Forex brokers have expanded the options chart and made it possible to trade with metals, indices, food, and other resources.

Moneyness—A technique used to define the correlation between equity in underlying cost and the strike amount of an option.

Morphing—The process of creating synthetic positions or transitioning from one position into another using a single order.

N

Naked call—happens when a speculator sells a call option on security without ownership of that security.

O

One-sided market—A market state when buyers are significantly more than sellers or sellers more than buyers.

Online brokers—A broker that allows you to process your orders through an online platform.

Opening order—An order used to create new options contract positions.

Options—Another financial derivative that, unlike futures and CFDs, is not affected by the price movement. To access the product, you simply pay a premium, and on the expiration date, the investor decides if they stay with the underlying derivative price or market price.

Optionable stock—A stock that acts as underlying security for certain options.

Options contract—A right to purchase or sell shares at specified strike prices and expiration times.

Options holder—The person who owns an options contract.

Options trader—A person who buys and sells options.

Out of the money—An option gets out of the money when the cost of the equity of the underlying security is not favorable to the trader based on the strike price. A call option can become out of the money if the value of the underlying equity is below the strike charges. On the other hand, a put option becomes out of the money when the cost of the underlying equity is higher than the strike charges.

Over-the-counter options—Options that are traded over the counter and not through online exchange platforms.

Overvaluing—An occurrence where a stock market trader estimates the prices of stocks to be higher than the actual value in the market.

Oscillators—Mathematical models applied to price action, based on some specific observation about market behavior. They are usually plotted below the stock chart, either as lines or histograms, and measure the strength of trends or movements in the price. When weakness in the trend is detected, it is suspected that it might be close to reversing.

P

Point or pip—A term used in the currency market to represent the smallest possible variation for a currency pair considered. Ex.: EUR/USD = 1,200, a fluctuation of 0.0001 equals 1 pip and for USD/JPY = 111.28, a fluctuation of 0.01 equals 1 pip.

Portfolio—A grouping of several financial assets such as currencies, cash, bonds, stocks, and other cash equivalents that are owned by an individual or an organization.

Position—A clear vision of an operator to buy or sell currencies; can also refer to the amount of currency which an investor owns.

Pricing model—A formula that can be applied in the determination of the abstract or theoretical value of a given options contract using variables such as the underlying security, strike price, and volatility.

Premium—The amount paid to acquire an option in the options market. Premiums are often quoted as price per share.

Profit—The excess revenue a stock trader gets from either buying or selling stocks in the stock market.

Physical option—The kind of option that has underlying equity in the form of physical assets.

Primary market—Treasuries are either public (countries) or private (companies) that issue securities for the first time before they can be traded on the stock exchanges.

Put option—An option that allows you to write or sell underlying equity at a specific strike amount and expiration times.

R

Realize a profit—Making a profit when you close a position contact.

Realize a loss—Incurring a loss when you close a position contract.

Renegotiation—When the settlement of the operation is extended to another date with the cost of this process based on the differential in the interest rates of the two currencies. A change overnight, specifically the next business day with respect to the next business day.

Retail trader—A person or an organization that is focused on investing their capital in futures, options, bonds, and stock.

Revaluation—An increase in the exchange rate of a currency established by other currencies or by gold.

Revaluation rates—The rate for any period or currency used to revalue a position or book. Rate revaluation is the rate used in the market when an operator runs an end-of-day to stabilize gains or losses on the day.

Risk—An unforeseen factor that can lead a stock trader to experience losses.

S

Scaling out—A situation in the stock market where a trader gets out of their position to either buy or sell their financial instruments.

Secondary market—Once the securities have been issued by the treasuries, they can be traded on local or international exchanges. These exchanges are known as the secondary market. Some examples are BVC, NYSE, NASDAQ, etc.

Securities—Any product negotiable in the stock market. Some examples are stocks, bonds, CFDs, Forex, futures, options, etc.

Security index—An indicator in the security market that uses statistical data to analyze the changes that are experienced in the securities market.

Sell to close order—An order placed when closing a long position that is already in existence.

Sell to open order—An order placed when opening a new contract position.

Settlement—When contract terms are finalized after exercising a position.

Share—An indivisible form of capital that is used to signify a person's ownership of a certain company.

Short—Some markets are deep enough to allow investors to sell products that they do not have, allowing them to obtain returns from falling prices. This means when you make a short belief that the market will fall and if your hypothesis is successful, you will earn money.

Short position—The state attained when you sell contracts.

Short selling—A phenomenon where a stock market investor borrows securities that they sell in the stock market to make a profit by buying them later.

Spread—A position made from selling several contracts belonging to the same underlying security.

Spread order—An order that instructs a broker to create a spread of several positions that are transacted simultaneously.

Stock—A type of security that gives individual ownership to a certain company and is sold at a particular market price.

Stockbroker—Those who advise investors in the purchase of securities from which they receive a commission. However, unlike traders, they do not operate in the market.

Stock market—A loose network of several traders who willingly buy and sell stocks that represent ownership of certain businesses.

Stock options—An agreement settled by the stock market investor and their broker granting the broker exclusive rights to buy or sell shares at a predetermined price.

Stock trader—An individual or a firm involved in the trading of stocks.

Stop-loss—A highly recommended practice in the stock market that consists of defining how much you are willing to lose in an investment. In practice, it is about saying if my losses reach X percentage (We do not recommend more than 1% per operation), I close the position before it hits my account considerably.

Stop-loss point—Points where a stock trader gives instruction of certain stocks to either be sold or bought when they attain a certain price in the stock market.

Stop order—An order implemented to close positions from the market when certain price parameters are attained.

Strike price—The amount of money given or received when a contract holder decides to close a contract position.

Swap—A derivative contract through which the parties involved exchange cash flows from two different financial instruments.

Swing trader— (Definition 1) A stock trader who holds their financial instruments, such as stocks, for a long time before they trade them.

Swing trader— (Definition 2) An individual who either buys or sells securities in the market for several days or weeks to capture the gains of the market.

Synthetic position—A trade position that combines options and stocks in a single contract to emulate another option position.

Synthetic long call—A synthetic position that allows you to own calls. It entails purchasing puts as well as their related underlying assets.

Synthetic long put—A position that allows you to own puts. It entails purchasing calls, then short-selling the underlying security related to the call.

Synthetic short call—A position that is similar to purchasing short calls. Entails selling stocks and selling put options associated with the stock.

Synthetic short put—A position that is similar to trading short puts. It entails purchasing stock, then selling call options associated with the stock.

Synthetic short stock—A synthetic options position that is similar to going short on stocks. It entails writing one call contract at the money, then purchasing one put option that is also at the money for the same underlying stock.

Support and resistance—Support is a price level below the current one in which the buying force is expected to exceed the sales force, so a bullish momentum will be slowed. Normally, support corresponds to a minimum earlier reached.

Resistance is the opposite of support. It is the price zone above the current one in which the sales force will exceed that of the purchase, ending the bullish momentum, and therefore, the price will tend to recede. Resistances are commonly identified in a graph as prior highs reached by the price.

T

Take profit—Many talks about the market going up or down; this is incorrect. The market moves down or up, that is, the market goes up and down all the time, but in a trend, a larger proportion of one of these movements prevails. Being aware that the market changes direction all the time, it is prudent to take profits from time to time since its direction or tendency does not remain eternally. We call this action to monetize benefits "taking profit."

Technical analysis— (Definition 1) A technique used to predict the price of financial instruments such as stocks through analyzing the historical price data of the underlying security.

Technical analysis— (Definition 2) A probability test whose result is the forecast of future price movements. It is the study of market action, mainly through the use of graphs, with the purpose of predicting future price trends.

Theoretical value—Refers to the cost of an option position derived using pricing models and mathematical formulas.

Time decay—The period when the extrinsic value of an option decreases as it approaches the expiration date.

Trading plan—A plan that traders create to outline how they will carry out transactions on the options market. The plan always contains objectives, trading methods, and strategies to be used.

Trailing stop order—An order whose stop price is a percentage change from the best price ever reached by a given position.

Trader—Any person who trades securities in the market with either their own money or someone else's.

Trading style—The method used by a trader when transacting on the options market.

Trend—A continuous movement or change in the price of options or market patterns.

Time value—The segment of the premium that is greater in value than the quoted intrinsic value.

U

Underlying asset—The base title on which derivatives are built.

Underlying stock—The kind of security upon which the value of an option is derived.

Undervaluing—A situation where prices of stocks are estimated to be lower than the actual market prices by a stock market trader.

V

Volatility—The level of rising or falling of the cost of a given option.

Vertical spread—A combination of options positions established from multiple contracts that feature diverse strike amounts with similar expiry dates.

Volatile market—An exchange platform that has prices or conditions that keep changing unexpectedly.

Volatility crunch—A sudden decline in an option has implied volatility.

Volume—The number of transactions carried out about a certain option or underlying security.

W

Weekly option—An option that expires within one week.

Writer—The person who creates contract positions for selling options.

Writing an option—The act of selling an option contract.

Conclusion

A high probability is that you are familiar with options trading. If you are not, then this article will provide an introduction into what options are. Hopefully, by the conclusion, you'll have a fundamental knowledge of what options are and how to trade them successfully."

Option trading is a derivative tool in equity investments where the buyer has two possible outcomes: they can either buy or sell an option to someone else. Options contracts must be bought or sold on specific exchanges through brokers who charge commission fees for execution. Individuals use these tools for a variety of reasons, including gaining more influence over the direction of their investments while reducing risk.

The party who has the right to buy or sell anything at a pre-determined price, known as the strike price, is known as the option holder. The term "option" is used to describe the contract that grants this right. The term "call" is used to describe a contract that enables its owner to BUY an underlying security and "put" is used for someone who can SELL an underlying security.

Since options give their holder rights and leverage, they also come with additional risk and cost associated with them. This makes it important for traders to understand what options are and how they work.

Let us say we have a call option at $100 on XYZ stock expiring in one month. If the stock is above this price at expiration, the call option holder has the right to purchase 100 shares of XYZ at $100 per share; if the stock is above this price at expiration, the call holder will exercise his right to purchase 100 shares at $100. If not, he can sell his contract for $100 which is the strike price. The cost to own this call option would be

$10 per contract or one-tenth of a penny. Traders place their orders in an options market by going through a broker who has become a member of an Exchange. These orders are then processed and executed by a pool of traders called "Market Makers".

Each time a trader buys or sells an option contract the broker charges them a small fee known as commission. This fee is often negotiated with the broker. The main difference between options and stocks is that options are bought or sold on an exchange, to be bought or sold at a specific price at a specific time, whereas you can buy or sell stocks without having to pay any commission.

The holder of a call has the right to buy the underlying contract at the strike price before expiration date. If the call is exercised, then he will have to buy it at that price. A put acts in similar way as a call, except that now the seller has the right to sell it instead of buy it.

A put option contract is a derivative security giving its owner a right to sell a fixed number of underlying assets at a fixed price on or before expiration date of that derivative security. The seller, or writer (right holder), is obligated by contract to deliver (make) the underlying assets if called upon by his counter party (call buyer). This obligating is called contract settlement.

Now that we have a basic understanding of what option trade, let's delve deeper into the scenarios that can be played out. There are three possible outcomes when an options trader exercises their rights depending on the price movement of the underlying "strike" asset:

BOOK 2

OPTIONS TRADING STRATEGIES

Advanced, Proven Techniques to Exponentially Grow your Money. Working Tips for Beginners And Specialists On How To Make Real Money With Options

"If you can't, you must. If you must, you can."

T. Robbins

Introduction

Options trading is a technique of buying and selling options to either speculate or hedge. They can be used to stabilize and do not demand an upfront payment like futures and therefore offer low leverage. Options may also be used as part of a larger investment strategy, such as the case with spreads, arbitrage, and straddles.

This article will discuss why options trading is essential to know the most common strategies for mastering them. It will teach you how to apply each approach to your portfolio in order to maximize market possibilities while reducing risk.

The first strategy will be to look at a simple example of a long call option. A long option gives the buyer the right to buy an asset at a predetermined price but not an obligation. A call option is a contract that gives you the right to purchase the underlying asset from the seller for a stated predetermined price called the strike price. If you have ever been interested in investing in real estate, then using options to hedge against this investment will help you take less risk. So instead of investing your entire life savings in a home outright, you can invest a smaller amount and use your savings as a down payment for the eventual house purchase. This also gives you the flexibility in terms of when you can buy the home without being locked in with a purchase contract.

When you are buying a call option, the value of the contract will determine how much of your investment you can use to find out what price is required for the house. For example, if you plan to purchase a 3-bedroom house for 150,000 dollars and have saved up 75,000 dollars deposited into your bank account, then an upside call option would have a value of looking at all qualities looking at properties that are close to this price range.

This call option contract is different from the standard stock options because they are not bought at the total price of the underlying asset. A short option gives the owner of an option the right to sell an asset at a specific price in the future. The best use of this strategy would be if you were planning on selling your stocks portfolio, but you are worried about how you would be able to do so promptly because your stocks have gone up in value in recent months, which makes your dividend up in value also. You could decide to sell some or all of your stocks by buying a short call which would give you control over when you will end up having to sell.

This method of investing is suitable for the investor because it allows them to lock in a price on the stocks that will be sold. Once the stock price drops, no further action will have to be taken. This strategy is used by people who are bullish on a particular stock but are afraid that it might end up dropping in value before they could sell them.

These strategies can help you maximize your profits and also minimize your risk exposure at the same time. If you educate yourself on what options trading is and how it works, you will be able to invest wisely and reduce your risk exposure by using these strategies.

Main Mistakes During Trading

There are many mistakes' traders make on a day-to-day basis. This article will highlight the main one's traders should be aware of, and some tips on how to avoid them.

Here are some of the mistakes that may happen:

- Not using indicators or using them incorrectly, which leads to overtrading

- Focusing on the short term, without setting long-term targets

- Taking rash decisions based on market price movements

- Being indecisive about trading methods, which leads to overcomplexity

- Buying or selling based purely on emotions or greediness etc.

These are just some things traders need to keep in mind when logging into their trading account each morning.

Traders should be sure to avoid these mistakes, as they will lead to more losses for the trader. Some traders have complained about losing money due to these simple mistakes, so it is important to avoid them.

It is very important for traders to set realistic targets. A trader should not want to aim at targets of 50% profit each month, because of this will lead to unrealistic expectations which are impossible for any trader that has just started trading. For example, if a trader had just started trading, that would expect him/herself of being able to double their profits every month. This is simply not possible without a lot of time and dedication.

The best way to set a realistic goal for a trader is to aim at 10% profit each month, whilst keeping an eye on the bigger picture. If a trader can double their profits each month from this target, then great! This shows that the basics of trading are being learnt quickly.

Another point that needs to be considered when setting targets is the amount of money that the trader has to invest into their trading account. It is often better to leave more money in case there are any unexpected problems with the account, instead of leaving only enough money for a few trades.

As well as setting realistic goals, it is important to keep the long term in mind. A trader who wants overnight profits will be extremely disappointed. Traders should look at the bigger picture and not simply look at the daily price movements.

There is also a lot of wisdom in keeping an eye on historical market trends, and keeping them in mind when trading. This is because over longer timeframes, the most common and profitable trend for a trader is upwards. Plain and simple: if a trader can learn to judge when a downtrend will start, they will be able to buy low and sell high with little difficulty.

Traders should also be very careful not to make rash decisions because of market price movements. Normally markets are driven by traders trying to make profits, which is what drives the market up and down. Traders who make rash decisions based on market movements risk losing big money because their trading strategy does not work out as planned.

Traders should be especially careful with trading methods; if a trader is unsure about which trading method, they should be using then it shows that the trader is indecisive and cannot cope with making important decisions. Since many traders are indecisive, this means that they will overcomplicate their trading strategy because of needing to check multiple websites for information about different methods, which can lead to overcomplexity.

Traders should be very careful with how they make decisions about whether to buy or sell an asset. Traders should ask themselves if the assets price is at a high or a low in relation to its historical trend. If a trader plans on buying many assets, but does not know in which direction the market will go, then they could lose a lot of money in the future because of not being able to predict where the market is going.

A trader may have strong emotions when they view an asset, and that may lead them to buy an asset when it would have been better to sell that same asset. Additionally, a trader may feel that he/she wants to sell an asset because of greed, instead of working out the best way to trade.

It is important for traders not to give in to their emotions. This is because emotions are not rational, so it is better for traders to use indicators on the charts when making trading decisions, rather than emotions. It is also important to focus on long term objectives instead of short-term profits.

As A Beginner, What Do You Need to Know?

The first thing a novice trader should learn about stocks is what they are. Stocks are common shares of ownership in a public company, and they represent partial ownership of that company. Brokers operate as middlemen between traders and buy-and-sell orders, allowing stocks to be bought and sold on the stock market.

The second thing to know is how the stock market works. The stock market is where companies sell their stocks for money (capital) that can then be used to grow their business or further expand it. They do so by opening up "shares" of ownership for purchase or sale within an established timeframe, called an "exchange. Shares are then traded between buyers and sellers with each party paying a "market price" for ownership in the company.

The final thing to know is how to invest in stocks. The most common way to invest in stocks is by using an online stock broker, who holds shares of ownership on behalf of investors and can buy and sell shares of ownership on their behalf. Investors can choose which stocks they want their broker to buy or sell for them, or they can choose to let the broker do it automatically by installing an "investment strategy" on their account that tells the broker how often and when they should buy or sell certain stocks.

Note: As a newbie, this article provides a quick overview of stocks. Learning how to invest in stocks, whether online or offline, is a subject that takes many hours of study and practice. Do not simply rely on this article as your sole source for learning about investing in stocks. A good online course on investing would be a good starting point for beginners, along with a local stock broker they can meet with face-to-face to learn more about investing in real life.

Risks And Benefits of Trading

One of the benefits of trading is that you can make profits without having to work too hard. The nicest thing about trading is that you don't need to be an expert in anything or know anything complex to perform it.

You only need a little know-how and a rudimentary understanding of how people think to get by in the long run.

Trading comes with its risks, though, so it's important to learn what those are before jumping right in with both feet. There are also many ways for people who want more advanced information than the basics on how to trade futures or other types of contracts.

If you decide to trade, you'll be trading a capital asset for a capital asset within the same sector, with both assets earning the same risk-free interest rate. You can also use futures or options to hedge non-cash assets such as commodities or real estate.

In addition to the risk of losing money, there are also risks associated with trading futures and swapping contracts. To get started, it's important to be familiar with these risks. If you don't understand what they are and how they function, you risk losing your hard-earned money on something that won't pay off for years, if not decades.

Risks of futures and swaps:

If the contract is not properly priced, you could end up with an unwarranted profit or unwarranted loss. You may make a profit if the futures price is higher than the cash price.

You may lose money if the futures price is lower than the cash price and you are unable to exit your position.

If your trade goes against you, it doesn't mean it's over. Instead, if market conditions change or other unforeseen events occur that work against your favor, you'll need to execute an adjustment. This can be done by reducing your position size or closing your position.

The futures exchange may not support trading all the listed futures contracts on the trading floor at the time you want to trade. You can't trade on margin if you don't have enough on deposit with the exchange. If you do, any gain on a contract would be offset by additional margin requirements for additional contracts.

The risk of an unintended transaction is another thing to watch out for.

You may want to track some of these risks because they go hand-in-hand with trading derivatives, which are futures and options that are linked to other derivatives that are based on underlying assets such as stocks or bonds, commodities or foreign currencies.

Ways to reduce trading risks:

1. Know where your money is.

You can't measure risk; you need to know what the potential loss could be on an individual contract, and be prepared to act accordingly. You can't say that some contracts are riskier than others unless you understand the potential loss associated with each type of contract. When assessing risk, some people look at probability of losing money; others look at how much money they'll lose if their trade doesn't work out as planned. It's critical not to mix together these two categories of dangers. Your goal should be to limit your potential loss so you can recover more than your original investment should your trade go against you.

2. Understand the risks.

You probably know the most common risks associated with trading a stock, bond, commodity or foreign currency. But not all futures and options contracts have equal risk. As you become more experienced at trading, you'll want to become familiar with the various types of futures and options contracts so you can better assess their risks.

3. Reduce exposure to leverage when selecting your trade size.

Take a look at what leverage is—and how it works—and make sure that you don't exceed your risk tolerance when using leverage in your trades. If you think you're going to be in a position that's too risky for your account size, don't use leverage in it. You can always use swaps or swaps-for-equity to break even.

4. Don't try to play the market.

You're probably thinking that since you're an experienced trader, you should be able to make money trading any way you want. This is true only if you do your homework. Even if you follow the correct methodology, it doesn't mean that your trades will turn out as expected every time. Always know how much risk you're taking on. If there's something missing about your plan, adjust it before taking the trade. You may find that it's better not to trade at all than take a trade that could go against you by accident or because of market conditions beyond your control.

5. Don't change your plan because of your past success.

Making money in the market is nice, but it's even better when you make good trades without taking too much risk. You should be aware that past performance is no guarantee of future results, and doing something that has worked in the past could end up not working in the future. If you're making money, stay with what works—and maybe even take smaller positions to reduce risk in case things turn against you.

6. Remember that this isn't a game; it's serious business—for both winners and losers.

It never seems to be enough, no matter how much money you have.

And it never seems to be enough, no matter how much money you lose. Although most people don't like to admit it, they're in the game because they want to be winners. If you're not careful, you could end up doing things that will make you lose more than enough money to support your lifestyle. Those who win big in the market sometimes win big in other ways—they get divorced, lose their health or make poor investments outside of trading. If your goal is to be a winner in the market and even larger winner outside of the market, knowing what wins are possible will help you stay away from unnecessary risks while trading.

7. Know your risk tolerance.

Knowing your risk tolerance before you make a trade will help you evaluate trades for size, goal and money management. Don't trade against your risk tolerance; instead, try to make the right moves every time. One of the biggest mistakes you can make is to go against what you know or believe in your gut. If your instincts tell you that it's not time to be trading—maybe because something happened in the market that changed it—don't be swayed by other people who are trading or who think it's time to be getting into or out of a position.

8. Remember that trends continue until they don't.

Markets are trend-following machines. This means that they tend to continue in one direction until something big happens to change them. This can happen in the form of news, economic reports or even sentiment shifts in the market. Trends tend to fluctuate, but will eventually end—and end quickly. While this is true for all markets, it's especially true with futures and options, which tend to move faster than stocks, bonds and commodities.

9. Understand what makes a market move.

As you look at how markets work, you'll see that anything that affects one market may move the entire system. This means there are times when the news you hear will move financial markets across the globe. And while you can't control what people say or think about what's happening in the world economy, there are still things you can do to help or hurt your trades based on your perception of what's happening in the world. The best thing you can do is to always be aware of what's happening worldwide, because it may affect your trading performance.

10. Understand that volatility has no relation to risk; risk is relative to how much money you're willing to lose.

Volatility and risk are often confused. Understanding volatility means you're more likely to adjust your trade based on how much it's going to move. Risk is something you can control, but it's different than volatility because risk is relative to how much money you're willing to lose on a trade. Whether or not something is risky depends on whether or not you will be able to handle the loss of your investment. If a trade goes against you and the market moves many times beyond your stop-loss point, it's not risky; it's devastating.

11. Know how far you can make money in one day and still break even over time.

As you get more experienced in trading, you'll start to figure out your risk tolerance and know the maximum return you can get on any one trade. You can then take calculated risks to achieve that profit if that's what your trade plan calls for. This is the key to making money in the markets—by understanding how much profit is possible on a single trade.

Risks associated with futures and options trading include short-term loss of capital, principal loss or extended periods of losing trades, which means everything traded outside of cash delivery can become worthless. There are also commissions involved with trading futures and options at times other than trading hours—for example, weekends or holidays—which can affect your ability to complete trades. Other risks associated with futures and options trading include the possibility of "phantom" or "black-box" orders, which are orders that you never received due to delays in the brokerage system.

Although the above are just some of the risks that are associated with trading futures, options or any other type of speculative investment, many individual investors have lost considerable sums of money (if not their entire investment) because they had no knowledge or understanding of the risks involved. Trading futures and options is not suitable for everyone. If you decide to trade these contracts, please make sure you understand all relevant risks before committing any funds.

No matter what strategies you choose to trade—or how often you trade—you always need a plan to help keep your trading on track. And, if you're trading futures and options for the first time, remember that they are different animals than stocks. Make sure you understand all of the risks involved with trading these types of speculative investments before you make any type of trade.

Fundamentals Of Technical Analysis

Getting into options trading requires that you institute trading strategies and practice level-headed, unemotional trading. There are no real 'secrets' to trading, nor is there anyone winning strategy that will work every time. The reason there is no specific strategy that works every time is that the market is changeable. This means that in order to trade well, a trader must be able to use a variety of statistical techniques. Without putting effort into using some of these statistical tools, the trader may as well put their choices up and throw a dart to select which they will trade on.

Chars

Good options platforms have some common tools that you will be able to use in making your prediction. The most prevalent of these is a chart of the asset you have selected. Now, as someone new to trading, these charts can be confusing, and often feel overwhelming, but the chart itself is a simple representation of the statistical data on the asset selected. How you choose to analyze this chart will depend on the complexity of it.

Let's start with what the option chain presents. The asset's price over a certain time period is displayed, and you can choose to see minutes, hours, days, or weeks ago. This gives the trader an insight into how much the asset has risen and fallen. Most platforms will allow you to see the opening high/low, as well as the closing high/low for each asset. This gives the trader an indication of how the asset's price has changed and whether there are any clear trends. The data displayed on these charts is called an option chain, and each option chain has two sections for calls and puts.

To set up your chart you will need to select the timeframe you want to view. Hourly and daily charts are not of any immediate use when making your prediction. Try to find a good mid-time frame of around four hours so that you can see how your selected asset has been fairing. At this point, you can select what format is easiest for you to read. I will break these down for you below, but most platforms will offer chart views as charts, bar charts, and candlestick charts.

Calculating Probability

Options trading is about probabilities and never about actually winning or losing. Because options are bound by time and conditions it becomes important to know how to calculate probabilities so that you can value your options. In other words, if the current price of oil is $65, what is the probability it will move either up, or down in the next hour. There are some factors in how to determine this probability which include;

- The volatility of the market. You will need to consider how volatile the market is, and if movement is enough to cross the strike price.

- The direction of the pricing. Is the pricing moving in a way that is favorable to your trade?

- The timing of your trade.

Your technical analysis and indicators will give you the answers to these probability factors.

Technical Analysis for Options Trading

The technical indicators in trading are used to predict what the market will do. This prediction is based on the patterns of the past. These indicators are used on graphs and charts to ascertain any past trends an asset has had in trading. This allows traders to make an informed decision on whether they should enter or exit a trade.

While there are several technical indicators that can be used for technical analysis in trading, some are more useful than others when entering options trading. The technical analysis required for options relies very heavily on indicators that can be applied to charts. These indicators show a pattern or trend in the underlying markets. These indicators fall into one of four categories.

Trend

Trend indicators show the market direction and are called oscillators.

Momentum

These indicate how strong a trend is as well as signaling where any reversals may occur

Volatility

Volatility indicators reflect how much a market moves and what the price variations are.

Volume

Volume indicators show the number of units that are sold and purchased. These are generally not necessary when trading NADEX because volumes do not influence the value of the contract's settlements. Having said that, they are a good indicator of the underlying market's price influence as a result of the volumes being bought and sold.

Top Indicators to Use

As I have established, technical indicators are pattern-based signals that are used to try and predict what the markets will do. Using these indicators can be overwhelming but choosing a few of these will help you to build a strategy that works for you.

Oscillators

As a technical analysis tool, oscillators show high and low bands between two extreme values. This indicates the trend of an asset between two bounds. Most traders use oscillators to determine short-term overbought and oversold assets. As an oscillator approaches the higher end of the band it is considered to be overbought and when it reaches the lower end, it is considered to be oversold.

When used in conjunction with other technical analysis methods, oscillators can greatly assist traders in deciding when to trade, when not to trade, and when to close early. The most common oscillators used are the stochastic oscillator, relative strength, rate of change, and money flow.

Pivot Points

Determining the price of an underlying asset helps to establish whether the asset will reverse its current direction. Options traders who understand the use of pivot points can protect themselves from losses by closing early or can use these pivot points to take advantage of any reversals in price. Veteran traders will tell you that pivot points help them to establish what direction an asset will go. These points show a specific point of support when a price supports itself as it falls, or resistance when the asset price meets resistance as it rises. In identifying these pivot points, the trader will have a better handle on what the predicted price movement will be.

Support and resistance levels are used in conjunction with specific pivot points to define the levels an asset's price will have difficulty overcoming. An example of support levels is gold has fallen through its pivot point and is on a downward trend. Having said that, the price of gold is expected to stabilize at its first support level. During trading, the support may hold, or it may not, in which case the price of gold will continue to fall. Resistance levels work opposingly. Let's say that gold is set to cross its pivot during an uptrend but slows before its first resistance level. The price may either breach or hold its levels, sending different signals to traders.

Candlesticks

Candlesticks are usually selected as the default analytical tool on most platform charts. They are displayed as long or short rectangular shapes and will vary in their lengths. Lines are displayed within these rectangles and are called wicks. If only lines are present, without the rectangles then you are viewing a bar chart that works on similar principles but is not as detailed. Each of these candles on your chart represents a timeframe. The longer the timeframe you have selected, the more candles will be shown on your chart. In other words, if you have selected a chart that displays the last four hours, each candlestick displayed will represent four hours.

The body of your candlestick is the rectangle, and the wicks are either white or green. If the wick is displayed as any other color it is known as a bullish candle or a candle that indicates the market was trending upwards at that specific time. A candle that is shown as black or red is a bearish candle or a market that was trending downwards during the

148

timeframe. The base and body of the candle will indicate the price of the asset at open and close of trade and the wick will let you know how high, or low the asset price reached during the timeframe.

Rules To Follow When Using Technical Analysis

With options technical analysis relying so heavily on technical indicators it becomes vitally important to apply your technical analysis to your charts and read this information correctly. The top five key indicators that options traders use include moving averages, average true range, moving average convergence/divergence, relative strength index, and stochastics.

Moving Average

Moving Averages are defined as trend indicators and assist traders in establishing the trend based on previous price actions. This data continually updates and new figures are available to traders as soon as they are available. Single moving averages (SMAs) are the easiest indicators to read and give the mean average of a group of indicator figures. Exponential moving averages (EMAs) use past data and are used to validate the most recent values. EMAs and SMAs are used alongside other trade indicators to help traders understand what is happening in the markets.

Average True Range

This indicator shows the volatility of the market. Also known as ATR, the higher the average true range is, the higher the market's volatility is. This ATR assesses the average price range of an asset over two weeks. Average true range indicators are extremely useful in trading options contracts as it shows how much the market may move. ATR cannot, however, tell you which direction the market will move or how high the

149

market volatility may be. While a highly volatile market may present a lot of opportunity for traders it also means that you will need to manage your risk.

Moving Average Convergence/Divergence (MACD)

As an indicator for market trends, the MACD consists of three trend indicators. These are the fast line, slow line, and histogram. Designed to show the relationship between two moving averages, MACD helps traders to identify new trends that may be forming. When two lines converge, a trend is forming, or, when the lines have crossed over each other a trend has reversed. MACD is particularly useful in ascertaining how a market will move and in which direction.

Relative Strength Index

Used as a momentum indicator, the relative strength index, or RSI shows whether the market has been oversold, or overbought. This data assists traders in deciding whether they want to buy or sell based on whether a trend looks like it will reverse. RSI is an anticipatory tool that helps traders to trade at the right time. For options contracts, a trader can use this indicator to decide whether to buy or sell based on the current trend momentum.

Bollinger Bands

Invented by John Bollinger, these bands define the upper and lower price range levels. These price ranges are plotted by the standard deviation's levels above and below the average moving price of an asset. These bands measure the distance of these price deviations by using two default values, being the period and standard deviations. These deviations are set to a value of 20 periods and 2 for standard, but you can choose to customize these combinations should you wish to. These bands are not meant to be used as a stand-alone tool and should be deployed with moving average data.

Intraday Momentum Index (IMI)

IMI is a great technical indicator for traders who trade frequently. It combines intraday candlesticks with RSI, giving a suitable range for day trading by showing oversold and overbought levels. As a potential trading opportunity tool, IMI can initiate bullish or bearish trades during an up or low trending market respectively. Traders calculate IMI by adding up the number of days trading and divided by the number of days trading plus the number of down days ISUP / (ISUP+IS Down), then multiplied by 100. Usually, traders will look at a 14-day time frame. Numbers of more than 70 indicate an overbought stock, whereas numbers less than 30 indicate a stock that is oversold.

Money Flow Index (MFI)

As a momentum indicator, MFI combines volume and price data. Usually measured over 14 days it indicates what trade pressure is in the market. Readings of over 80 are an indicator of a market that is overbought, while numbers under 20 show an oversold market. MFI is usually used to track stock-based trades and long-term trades. MFI data that moves in the opposite direction to the stock price shows a trend change.

Put Call Ratio (PCR)

Used to measure trade volumes, PCR measures the change in the market's sentiment. More puts than calls with a ratio above 1 shows a bearish market, while a ratio that shows a call volume of less than 1 indicates a bullish market.

Open Interest (OI)

Open interest shows the amount of open or unsettled options contracts. OI does not show upward or downward trends but can be an indicator of how strong a trend is. Open interest trends that are increasing are indicative of new capital inflow, which in turn sustains a current trend.

Basic And Intermediate Strategies

Of course, there are very complicated going long strategies that can be employed, but it is best to start simply and get a lay of the land as a beginner.

Buying Calls, The "Long Call"

This strategy is considered by options traders who want to profit from an asset that increases in the price above the strike price. This is often considered so that the trader does not have to buy the asset outright to potentially profit without taking on the major risk of owning that asset.

This type of option can also afford the trader access to assets they cannot afford to purchase at that time. This is a common practice in accessing stock. Having the option to purchase is less expensive than purchasing the stock outright.

Here is a summary of how a long call works:

Outlook: Bullish.

Risk: The premium paid.

Potential profit: Unlimited. It increases as the price of the asset increases.

Break-even price: The sum of the strike price and premium paid (strike price + premium paid).

An example of a successful long call is as follows:

An options trader buys 100 shares of stock that he believes will increase in value within the next few months. Each share costs $20. He believes the shares will go up by at least $10. Therefore, he buys the option at a strike price of $20 plus a cost of $2 for each stock, which totals $22 per stock.

As long as the stock goes above $22, this long call option is profitable to the trader. For every dollar the stock goes higher, the trader will profit $100. As the stock price increases, so does the option value. Therefore, the trader can sell the option to lock in his profit.

The best thing about such an option is that the asset can infinitely increase in value, leading to massive profits. This is why long calls are a popular way to bet on rising stock prices.

In this case, this is also a risk that the trader will lose their investment in the cost of the premium and associated fees. The asset may not become advantageous before the expiration date arrives and thus, the option becomes worthless to the trader.

Buying Puts the "Long Put"

This option allows the trader to sell the underlying asset at the strike price on or before the expiration date.

As a result, the options trader profits when the asset's price falls below the strike price.

As you can see, this is similar to a long call, except the trader is betting on the asset's value falling below the strike price on or before the expiration date.

Long puts are a great way of protecting the value of assets that you already own.

Here is a summary of how a long call works:

Outlook: Bearish (Falling prices).

Risk: The premium paid.

Potential profit: Unlimited. It increases as the price of the asset decreases.

Break-even price: The difference between the strike price and premium paid (strike price - premium paid).

An example of a successful long put is as follows:

A company is trading stock at $50 per share. An options trader feels that this price will fall to at least $30 per share within the coming months and so, seeks a put option with a strike price of $50 that had an expiration date of 2 months. He buys 100 shares and pays $150 to purchase each $50 share. The option is priced at $5 per share and so, the trader pays $500.

The trader was right, and the stock price depreciates to $25 per share before the expiration date. With the current stock price, the trader with the put option will be in the money because the stock's intrinsic value has risen. Let's say that this value is now $1500. The trader can sell the stock for that price. The trader will make a profit of $1000 after removing his investment of $500.

The great advantage in this scenario is similar to the advantage in the long call, hence why this too is a popular way of betting on declining stock values. As a result, a long put is a great option if the trader expects the asset's price to fall significantly before the expiration date arrives. However, if the price falls only a little or not at all, the trader may be in the money only slightly, which is not profitable, or worse, it may not even return the premium the trader spent.

The long position in options trading refers to the fact that the investor owns the asset associated with the option. This is comparable to the short position, where the investor does not own the asset being associated with the option.

Regarding options trading, the long position refers to whether or not the trader will hold a long call or long put option. Again, this is dependent on the associated asset attached to that contract. Holding a long call option means that the trader expects that the asset's price will go up to benefit in that regard. If that upward trend is fulfilled, the option allows the trader to buy that asset at the strike price.

With a long-put option, the trader expects the asset to depreciate to purchase the right to sell that asset at a predetermined price.

While this can be disadvantageous in that there is no guarantee the advantage will be realized by the expiration date and this is a risky move in the short-term, the benefits include:

• Having a locked strike price even if the profits grow beyond expectations.

• The losses are limited.

• This move can rely on historical data to maximize profit.

• Using both the long call and long put strategies can be highly advantageous to options traders.

Covered Call Strategies in Depth

Also known as a buy-write, this describes the act of selling the right to purchase a specified asset that you own at a specified price within a specified amount of time, which is usually less than 12 months. It is a two-part strategy whereby someone first purchases a stock then sells it at the share-by-share prices.

The beauty of this type of option is off the bat, the seller benefits by receiving a premium payment from the options holder. Risk is mitigated because the seller already owns the stock. Therefore, your costs are covered if the stock price rises above the strike price. You simply deliver as agreed and rip any further rewards if the trader chooses to exercise the right to purchase on or before the expiration date.

Stock is the most common asset used in this type of option.

If you choose to consider covered calls, you need to be willing to own the stock at your price even if the price depreciates. Remember that there is no guarantee that you will earn greatly on the stock you have purchased due to the volatility of financial markets. Therefore, you need to be diligent in your focus on seeking good quality stocks that you are willing to own. In addition, you need to still potentially benefit from that ownership if there are down periods in the market.

As the seller of a covered call option, you need to be also willing to part with that stock if the price rises. You cannot change your mind if the stock price goes up if you have already entered into an option with a willing buyer. You must exercise that delivery if the trader chooses to exercise that option.

The maximum potential profit of covered calls is achieved if the stock price is met at or above the strike price of that call at or by the expiration date. The formula for this is as follows:

Sum of the Call Premium + (Strike Price - Stock Price) = Maximum Potential Profit

The seller also needs to consider the break-even point at the expiration date. The formula for this is as follows:

Purchase Price of the Stock - The Call Premium = Break-Even Analysis

The seller also needs to determine the maximum risk potential. This is equal to the purchasing price of the stock at the break-even point.

The seller also needs to be satisfied with the static rate of return and the if-called rate of return on the stocks. The static return is the approximate annual net profit of a covered call, assuming that the stock price does not change until the expiration date and until the option expires. To calculate this value, the seller needs to know:

- The purchase price of the particular stock.

- The strike price of the option.

- The price of the call.

- The number of days until the option expires.

- If there are any dividends and the amount of these dividends.

Calculating these factors leads to a percentile figure being determined. The formula for calculating this is:

(Call + Dividend) / Stock Price × Time Factor = Static Rate of Return

The if-called return is an approximate annual net profit on a covered call with the assumption that the stock price is above the strike price by or on the option's expiration and the stock is sold at expiration. To calculate this figure, which is also a percentage, the same factors need to be determined. The formula for calculating this is:

(Call + Dividend) + (Strike − Stock Price) / Stock Price × Time Factor = If-Called Rate of Return

Benefits of Covered Call Options

The first benefit of covered call options is the seller receives a premium payment, which can be kept as income whether or not the trader chooses to exercise the right to the option. This can be set up as a regular cash flow by serious investors in relatively neutral or bullish markets. Second, the investor can set up a program for selling covered calls regularly. This can potentially set up a monthly or quarterly income stream.

The second benefit of covered calls is that they can help investors target a selling price for a stock above the current price. Lastly, covered calls have the additional benefit of limiting risks as the asset protects the seller.

Risk And Rewards of Covered Calls

The first major risk of covered calls is that the seller can lose money if the stock price depreciates below the break-even point. This is a risk that anyone who owns stock takes on.

The second risk is not being able to anticipate a huge price rise in the stock price. Stocks have unlimited profit potential, but if the holder of the options for that stock chooses to exercise their right, the seller has to hand it over to this person. This can lead to a great missed opportunity as the seller has to hand over a tremendous asset in the transaction.

Advanced Trading Strategies

Levels (1-10)

One of the most essential aspects of trading is that the quality of your work varies depending on how much you trade. The more you trade, the better your chances of profiting. Below are some potential costs and rewards associated with different levels of trading experience:

Level 1 - Trading one contract per week on either side of Atlantic from home computer with market data from broker.

Level 2 - Trading two contracts per week in same fashion as Level 1 but using a deeper understanding of risk management in portfolio.

Level 3 - Trading 10 or more contracts per week in real time from home. Uses multiple tools and indicators.

Level 4 - Trading 10 or more contracts per week in real time from home, sometimes as much as 100 - 200 contracts per day (more than 50% of total world market). Uses multiple tools and indicators.

Level 5 - Trading 10 or more contracts per week in real time from home, sometimes as much as 100 - 200 contracts per day (less than 50% of total world market), using multiple tools and indicators for mechanical and discretionary strategies.

Level 6 - Professional trader trading full-time for a firm, either at the exchange or for an institutional investor. A trader must be able to trade numerous contracts every day, either manually or through a platform, in order to accomplish this.

Level 7 - Institutional trader trading multi-contracts per day from home, using multiple tools and indicators.

Level 8 - Institutional trader trading multi-contracts per day from home, using multiple tools and indicators for mechanical and discretionary strategies.

Level 9 - Professional trader trading full-time at a major investment bank. A trader must be able to trade numerous contracts every day, either manually or through a platform, in order to accomplish this.

Level 10 - Professional trader trading full-time at a major investment bank. In order to do this, a trader should be able to trade multiple contracts per day manually or using a platform, using multiple tools and indicators for mechanical and discretionary strategies.

How To Improve Your Trading Level

Your trading level is the most important thing when it comes to becoming a successful trader. It's the most important because this will determine your level of profitability. However, not many people know how to increase their trading levels or where to even start! This article will give guidelines on how you can improve your trading level and become a better trader in just six simple steps."

This article will provide you with 6 easy-to-follow steps on how to improve your trading level. These steps are broken down by providing an overview on each step, followed by more information on what they entail on the bottom of the page.

By improving their level of trading, traders will be able to achieve more consistently higher profits.

Step 1: Identify Your Strengths and Weaknesses

Identify your strengths and weaknesses. Clear perception on your strengths and weaknesses are critical to the trading process. Many people tend to think that they're good at trading, but often aren't able to prove that by consistently winning at the markets. There are some things you are undoubtedly better at than others, so it's important that you know what you're doing well before trying new things.

For example, if your best trading skill is to know when to buy and sell, you need to identify the times you do that best. Instead of just jumping into a trade you might want to note down all of your trades and figure out why most of them were winners or losers.

On the other hand, maybe you're not as good at buying and selling but you're really good at analyzing charts and predicting where price is going next. If this is the case, concentrate on honing your charting abilities and properly analyzing markets before entering a trade.

Step 2: Find Investors Who Are Interested in Your Skillset

Find people who are interested in your skillset and that know that you're trying to improve so they can provide you with support. That means by finding people who want to work on the same things as you, such as those who love trading and those who aren't so confident at it. Such people can provide support for each other and work more efficiently together than those with different interests.

You may be thinking of asking your local banker but you can still find people who would be interested in working on trades with you. For example, there are those who love trading and those who aren't so confident at it and today's economy is all about the people that don't know what they're doing. When one of them learns how to trade and builds up their skills, they will help more people by showing their examples and strategies through video lessons.

If you don't feel like asking your local banker at first, you can always look for other cities on the internet. For example, you could search for local forums on trading and if you find one that is active, join it. There you can get picked up by like-minded individuals and make new friends along the way.

Step 3: Get Sure That You Have the Right Skillset and The Time

First of all, your time at home before going to work is probably the most important time you have in a day. And you should know what exactly you want to do with that time. For example, if you want to spend it trading, make sure that you can make enough money in a day to cover your expenses and still have some spending money left over. As a starting point, it is recommended that you try and trade with at least $1,000 of your own money and never risk more than 1% on a particular trade.

Next is the right skillset. If you're not sure what your skillset is yet, you can think of it as being "your formula" for trading. You have the right skillset if your formula is simple and easy to do.

It should be easy to understand, so you should be able to explain it to someone else in a short period of time. Most importantly, your trading skill should match up with your interest, so that it should be an enjoyable thing for you that you want to do whenever possible.

If trading is something that makes you enjoy yourself during the day, then it should be something that will keep happening over time. If not, then let it go.

Step 4: Find the Time to Practice Your Skill

Once you know your strengths, weaknesses, the time you have to trade and the money you can trade with, all that's left is practicing to perfect your skillset. For example, if you're interested in practicing but your best skill is still at home while you're working then try practicing during lunch break. Or if your best skill is charting then leave an hour or two to study that while at work.

Practice the same way every day so your body gets used to it more quickly. It's easy to get distracted by emails, calls or urgent tasks so set an alarm on your watch or phone to remind you. Then you can remind yourself that you're not there to work; you're there to practice.

It doesn't matter what time of day or night you practice as long as it is during your free time and you make sure that there are no distractions around. If the urge comes, fight it away by reminding yourself of what's waiting for you if you give in.

Step 5: Find A Way to Keep Your New Skills Up

Once you find a way to keep your new skills up, it's important that you stick with it. For example, if you're in a place where there are no trading books available in the library then just bring in an electronic copy. All that matters is that you can refer back to it anytime when your trading needs you. And if you're not sure how well your skills are developed then spend time with others who are at the same level as you are.

Step 6: Keep Practicing and You'll Be on Your Way to Becoming a Better Trader

Keep practicing your skills over time. If you're not sure how well your skills are developed then spend time with others who are at the same level as you are. For example, if you're interested in trading then find other traders to learn from. There are plenty of good ones out there that want to help people that are very willing to teach, so don't hesitate to ask them for their advice.

Beware of scams. Most of the people who want to help you out are not out to take your money. If you ask them, they will always tell you that they are working to help others and not looking to profit from you. They won't promise that "one day" they will be rich but all they want is for you to continue trading with their help.

If someone offers "unfair methods" or tries to sell you anything that may work against your instincts, then just ignore them and move on. There are plenty of good traders out there that are willing to help you anyway.

Q&A To Help You Get Most Out of Trading

Why is it better to trade in Options than other forms of investing?

Investing in options is often looked at as a complicated task which requires an experienced professional with access to strategic resources. These experts are able to trade in options on the stock market with leverage funding, which allows them to invest more capital than they can afford. This can also allow them to make quick profits when stocks reach higher levels, but it is important for investors not to lose money when the reverse happens.

How can I limit my losses?

In order to effectively limit our losses from trading, we have to understand how they work within the greater picture. At its core, losses are simply a function of time. Since every trade has a predetermined time limit, whether it's 6 months, 6 days or 6 hours, if we don't have enough knowledge to handle trading with our head up in the air, staying in a losing trade doesn't really change anything.

You see, with each passing day that your account loses money, you're getting chipped away at by time. Once you hit that point where your account is down 25%-50%, you know that you're close to having to cut your losses and stop trading. At this point most traders would consider taking profits and moving on to another strategy.

Differences Between Puts and Calls

A put option holder has the option, but not the obligation, to acquire a set number of shares at a specific price. Put options can be used to hedge against a drop in the stock market.

Call options provide holders the opportunity to buy a given number of shares at a specific price within a specified time period before they expire or are exercised (e.g., three months). Call Options can be used as an investment tool because they offer potential for significant growth if their underlying stock price goes up and/or if their expiration date is reached before that time period expires (the shares will automatically go out-of-the-money then).

Assets Can I Trade-In?

Many people are looking to trade-in different assets, but there are certain assets which you cannot trade in because they would be considered "smart". The article will provide guidance on what is and isn't eligible for trade-in.

Trading in any asset that goes over 20% of the price paid by someone cannot be done. Additionally, limited edition items cannot be traded in for cash or prizes. Some assets may not be eligible due to their limited nature, such as game tickets or airport lounge access. This article will provide guidance on various items that no longer contain their original packaging which means they could not have been bought with cash or prize money.

Can I Trade in Options Even If the Market Is Going Down'?

Before you get too worked up over what's going on with your portfolio, double-check that everything is legal. While there are some gray areas with trading (i.e., is it legal or not?), there are certain things that are definitely not allowed by law. Without knowing this information beforehand, any investor could be taken advantage of if they're unaware of what's already on the books today. In the following article, we'll examine what options you have open to you when the market is going down.

Is It Safe to Invest in Options?

Many people will say yes because they seem like such an easy way to make money. In reality though, these trades can be very risky and lead investors into financial ruin.

The risks to be aware of for options trading are that the company's stock price may either increase or decrease drastically. If you invest in an option, you are basically investing in pure speculation, making it highly risky. Purchasing an option is similar to purchasing a lottery ticket in that there is no certainty that your investment will pay off.

Money Management

Effectively dealing with your capital and risk exposure is basic when trading options. While risk is unavoidable with any type of investment, your exposure to risk doesn't need to be an issue. The trick is to manage risk funds well; make sure you're comfortable with the level of risk you're taking and that you're not taking on too much risk.

Similar ideas can be applied while dealing with your money as well. You ought to be trading utilizing capital that you can afford to lose; abstain from overstretching yourself. As effective money and risk management are completely vital to fruitful options trading, it's a subject that you truly need to comprehend. We will take a look at a portion of the techniques you can, and should, use for controlling your budget and managing your risk exposure.

- Managing Risk with Options Spreads

- Managing Risk Using Options Orders

- Managing Risk through Diversification

- Using Your Trading Plan

- Money Management & Position Sizing

- Using Your Trading Plan

It's imperative to have a nitty-gritty trading plan that spreads out rules and parameters for your trading exercises. One of the pragmatics uses of such a plan is to assist you in dealing with your money and your risk exposure. Your plan ought to incorporate details of what level of risk you are OK with and the amount of capital you need to utilize.

By following your plan and just utilizing the money that you have explicitly distributed for options trading, you can keep away from probably the greatest mix-up that traders and investors make: utilizing "scared" money.

When emotion assumes control over, you possibly begin to lose your concentration and are obligated to behave irrationally. It might make you pursue losses from past trades turned sour, for instance, or making transactions that you wouldn't generally make. If you follow your plan and stick to utilizing your investment capital, then you should have a greatly improved potential for the success of monitoring your emotions.

The Basics

We're all familiar with the woes of trying to save money at some point in our lives but it can be difficult when we are always given more tasks than hours in a day or seem like there never seems like there is enough money coming in. With money management and savings, we want to make sure that we have enough money to spend on ourselves and our loved ones while also being able to save enough to meet our financial objectives. It's important to take control of your spending and ensure you are receiving more than what you are giving so you don't go into debt or let your money escape your control. Nothing is more frustrating than being in debt because you didn't know how to manage your money properly. Money, on the other hand, makes no distinction between those who are financially well-off and those who are not. It can happen to anyone.

To take charge of your finances, you must understand the fundamentals of how money is invested, saved, and spent. Your approach to money should also be determined by your goals in life; if you're looking for financial security or retirement in the next 10 years or so, then start putting your money away in savings accounts and make sure you are getting a good interest rate on them (5% is pretty sweet) but if you are looking for ways to spend more time with your family while still being able to pay off some debt then it may be best to get a loan on a new car or have an emergency fund of ready cash that can help you escape any debt that may arise.

Advantages And Disadvantages

Advantages

-No more worrying about where your money is going.

-Money can be saved to the account you choose, freeing up a checking account for specific types of expenses.

-The best way to manage your finances and find specific information about transactions is online with a debit card, credit card, etc.

Disadvantages

-It can be hard to keep track of all your spending as there may not always be paper trail as in cash.

-Payments for bills or subscriptions will need to be made via debit card or credit card making it harder to stay within budget limits.

-It's important to make sure your bank or financial institution has safeguards in place to prevent unauthorized use of your card.

-You may be required to carry a credit card at all times, which can be inconvenient.

-You are not limited to one account, you are given the option of adding, removing, or making changes to accounts at any time.

-If your card is lost or stolen you are liable for any charges that are made.

-Some financial institutions may charge fees for having additional accounts in addition to monthly fees for each account you have with them. You may also need proof of identity in order to open an account with them in the first place.

Why Is It Important?

There are many reasons why it is important to have good money management skills. The most obvious reason being so you can keep track of your expenditures and build an emergency fund with savings in case anything happens. Other reasons include the ability to budget effectively so that there's always enough money for what's needed, being able to help others with financial needs when they arise because of empathy for others' situations and decreased natural desire to spend money on oneself because it will be there when needed.

The key to good money management skills is one of the keys to happiness. If you ask anyone who is successful with money how they became so, they'll tell you that it was because they focused on managing their money. They would make a budget and stick to it, saving for things that were important to them which would be outlined in their budget. As time went on, what made them happy was spent on what made them happy. Every time they bought something or did something else, they learned something. Money management was not always about making money for yourself but also making more of what you already have by investing it wisely and drawing lessons from those investments.

Risk Management

It is vital to be fully aware of the risks associated with trading. There are different types of risks you should consider when trading; behavioral, technical and fundamental.

Behavioral and Technical Risk: These two types of risks come into play when you talk about your overall risk-taking ability and how much you can afford to lose on any particular trade. This is something that is hard to control, but you need to take into consideration. This would include how much risk you're willing to absorb on any particular trade, as well as how big of a position (and thus how much money) you're taking. Understanding this will give you a larger understanding of your investment strategy and assist in building your trading system.

Fundamental Risk: The third type of risk involves the underlying asset or market structure itself. Markets can be volatile and unpredictable. Fundamental risks can be caused by economic news, regulatory changes, changes in the laws concerning the U.S., political shifts or even just random external events that could cause markets to act different than expected.

When trading, you have to be aware of which risks are associated with the individual trade, not just with your position overall. This is knowing your risk tolerance.

Risk tolerance is how much potential money you could lose on any single trade. Risk tolerance includes how much money you are willing to lose on an entire position if necessary.

Risk management is the process of controlling these various risk factors in order to maximize gains and minimize losses in trading. Traders should know their own risk tolerances, both in terms of how they handle losses and what percentage gain is necessary for them to feel that a trade was worth the investment.

There are two basic ways to manage your investment background and the size of your position:

1. Stop loss: This will ensure that you do not lose more than a specified percentage of any given trade, and it will help you to take less risk overall.

2. Fixed-position sizing: This is the opposite of a stop loss. If you use this style of risk management, your position sizing (how much money is put into one trade) will be the same regardless if the market has gone up or down, or how much volatility is present in the market. With this method, you run no risk of having unrealistic stop losses and losing big if things go wrong and you don't cut your losses quick enough.

There are many ways to control risk; some traders focus on one aspect while others grab all the tools they can get. Here are few examples of how you should incorporate risk management into your trading styles:

A common way of managing risk in trading is to use stop loss orders. Set a stop loss order that divides your capital into two positions: what you're willing to lose and what you're willing to keep. Once your position goes below this level, it's placed immediately, either all at once or in parts. Then if it were to go above this level, an alert is sent out so that you could quickly get back in or exit the trade. For a stop loss order to be effective, you must remember to place the order well before the market fluctuates significantly downward or upward.

A trailing stop is another option. With this method, instead of setting a fixed point at which you want your position closed, you set a percentage distance from the latest high or low. When it's reached, an alert is sent out so that you can decide whether or not to close the trade. This method has been found to have lower success rates than a standard stop loss. The reason for this is that if a stock makes a few quick swings back and forth before going up, your initial stop will be triggered by each mini-swing.

Another way of risk management is to use a limit order. This involves placing an order for a future trade that will only take place at a specified price. A stop loss can be used as a form of limit order, but the main difference is that with a limit you have to wait for your desired price before entering a trade, whereas with a stop loss you can enter the trade as soon as it reaches your desired price range.

A final way of risk management is to use stops based off volatility at certain times during the day. This method involves putting stop losses at key times during the day when volatility may increase or decrease.

Diversification of Risk

In markets, there is always a need to diversify risk. Thus, in trading, the entry into a position must be in accordance with this idea.

This is not something that can be achieved in one day - it takes time and effort since you would want to build up your capital but also ensure that you do not lose too much in doing so. Therefore, the strategy for this takes some time due to the fact that it has to overcome obstacles like; financials; psychological; trade-related; economic; and legal risks.

It requires planning which is why diversification of risk is hard but when completed successfully can yield good returns for both traders and investors alike.

The first step of risk diversification is to have a goal. This will be helpful in measuring your success and progress, and it will also allow you to decide if you are going the right direction.

Another advantage of having a goal is that it can help you overcome your anxieties. Set very high goals if you want to get something from trading, but keep in mind that even reaching just half of your goals would already be quite an achievement.

You should not be afraid to take risks since this is the whole point of trading, however don't take too much that you wouldn't be able to cope up with it when loss sets in.

It's crucial to consider your aim since you don't want to find yourself in a scenario where you're trapped with money you can't use once you start losing.

Also, do not close your eyes when the market goes down; this will only inflict more damage on your portfolio. On the other hand, if you hold on in spite of the fact that you are downing in value, do not panic and keep calm because this will be beneficial for you in the long run.

Having a clear goal allows traders to prepare for each step-in order to protect themselves throughout their trading day. Most traders start by opening a long and short position.

To prevent them from losing too much and hurting their account and trades, they should be sure that they will be able to handle the later stages. They can do this through proper risk management.

They should also know what they are doing; those who don't know how properly manage positions may end up making mistakes which could towards serious losses. Understanding risk will also allow them to make better decisions as time goes on since it will help them pinpoint their problem areas as well as help them find a solution – this is based on an analysis of their situations.

Most importantly, when in doubt, it is important for traders to stop and think before they act. This will give them time to think about what could happen if they make a wrong decision; this will also allow them to make the right decisions in the long run.

The second step in diversifying risk is to know which position to open based on the goal that you set for yourself. You may want to trade several markets or just one today, but if you are not sure of what you're doing, you're bound to experience losses.

It is important to know that this is one of the ways that you can be successful in the long run; you could trade in different markets and open up an account in each of them.

Also, when diversifying risk, you should spread it out over a period of time; this will allow your trades to grow and they will match your goals.

How To Become a Top Trader?

Strategies

There are many strategies to becoming a top trader. This article will go through many aspects of trading, including the three most important skills, emotions in trading, and more!

Many people want to be that one trader who has it all. It sounds like an impossible goal but it is possible to become a top trader with some hard work and knowledge about what it takes. Trading can be profitable but also risky which is why having the right mindset is key. There are many ways to get the right mindset but the most important being able to manage your emotions while trading during unfavorable periods or prices fluctuating up or down in rapid movements.

Another important skill to have been being able to choose the ones that are right for you. When choosing a strategy, it's important to know what type of trader you are. There are three main types of traders: Day trader, Swing Trader, and Position Trader. If you're new to trading then day trading can be risky but can also be very profitable. The same goes with swing trading which is why these two types of traders should be avoided by beginners until they get a hang of things.

Position Traders are generally more experienced and know how to manage their emotions when things turn sour and also know when it's time to get out at the top.

The best way to become a top trader is to learn from other top traders. Finding a mentor is the best way to learn and it's also priceless. A mentor can teach you not only what it takes to be a successful trader, but also teach you the right mindset, the right strategy, and what not to do so you can avoid mistakes and losses.

Some of these mentors will even give you access to their personal trading accounts so that you can see what they see and learn from them in real time. This is extremely helpful in learning about the market behavior and how they read it which is huge in becoming a top trader yourself.

There are many ways to becoming a top trader but these are some of the most important. You may achieve the level of trading that many people dream about if you can control your emotions, adopt the correct approach for you, and find a mentor to teach you what they know.

Mindset

When I first started out as a binary options trader, I put a lot of attention on education. Outside of the normal statistics and research, I wanted to know what it meant to be a trader. If one chose to believe most of the binary options adverts on the internet, you would think that all binary options traders were self-made multimillionaires who took mere weeks or months to accumulate their wealth. I am not denying that making a large sum of money off of binary options is impossible, nor am I saying that it must take a long time. It is simply that these millionaire traders are the outliers. Think of it like people who play casino slots. Hundreds of thousands of people will play these slots daily, with only two or three taking home the jackpot in a day. Experienced traders understand that binary options trading requires work, and involves some form of risk as well as an element of luck. Having said that, luck is not the only factor to consider when trading, as I was soon to learn. No trader is immune from the psychological aspects involved in any form of stock market trading. It took time and enormous amounts of discipline to not get sucked into the highs and lows that the stock market induces in people.

At first, I found trading binary options a little stressful. I, like so many other novice traders, allowed my emotions to dictate many of my trades. Because new traders often fall into the trap of presuming that binary options trading is easy, quick money because of the yes/no nature of the trade, they can become disappointed or disillusioned with trading quickly. The truth is, a winning trade does not equal a losing trade, nor does it cancel out any losses. In understanding that I was going to receive a percentage of my premium returned for a winning trade, and risking my entire premium for a losing trade, I began to gain a better grasp on what it would take to become a successful trader. Understanding the transparency as well as the concept of winning in percentages prepares the mind for thinking in statistical probabilities, and binary options trading is exactly that, a game of statistical probabilities. Once your mind begins to think in a statistical way, it is easier to detach yourself from the emotions that come with trading. Instead of fearing a loss, I began to control my decisions based on the reliable information and data that I had gathered. Added to this, I let go of the dollar amount I wanted to make, substituting this for the percentage I wanted to attain. Knowing that binary options was about long-term gains produced with short-term profits immersed me deeper into my trades.

With the veritable treasure trove of statistical data, strategies, analyses, and charts available to me for free, I dove deep into knowledge gathering, but something was still missing. I didn't understand what it was that made a trader successful and what did not. All of the insights, charts, and analysis tools out there would make no difference to my trades if I did not change my mindset to that of a trader. I found that most new binary options traders had, probably from those unscrupulous internet adverts, developed an inflated expectation of what trading binary options could do for them. A foul taste in their mouth has been left by misguided huge trades, bogus broker appraisals, and an inability to trade without emotion. So, what distinguishes a great trader's thinking from that of others?

Personal Advice from a Professional Trader

You must learn from the successful traders that have come before you to prevent catastrophic losses along your trading journey. Before each trade, ask yourself how likely it would be for you to recommend this trading on this contract to others. Should the expiry time, trade amount, or asset be doubtful on any aspect of your criteria, do not place the trade yourself. The moment you start to compromise your own values or beliefs to place a trade, you are losing. Stay focused and calculated with your risks, never wavering from your planned spend. Making arbitrary money management decisions increases your risk and leads to less predictable results for your trades. If you still find yourself gravitating towards a higher wager, ask yourself why you feel this trade warrants a greater investment. While it is extremely rare that a trade justifies a higher investment, sometimes you may choose to take a chance.

Should you decide to wager a much larger trade, check your broker's terms and conditions carefully. A trade that offers an early closure option may help to mitigate the risk of a greater investment amount. Monitor your trade very carefully and if you feel that the trade is moving against you, exercise your right to close early on the trade. If you aren't sure whether to close early or not, ask yourself whether the original reasons for trading the higher amount no longer exist. If these reasons do not exist anymore, cut your losses or take your lesser profit and get out of the trade. When a deal appears to be moving against you, it's a good idea to trust your instincts. Should your trade move against you and there is no early closure, you will need to accept the loss, but be prepared to analyze what went wrong. Taking some time away from the trading desk, then coming back to analyze what went wrong will help you to ascertain if there is anything you could have done to change your trade. Once in a while, you may have a trade that inexplicably closes out-of-the-money, but most times analysis will guide you to what went wrong. Usually, breaking your trade rules will be the primary reason for a losing trade. Make sure to note what your reasons for losing were and try not to repeat this behavior.

Finally, ensure that you have a mindset checklist. Go through this checklist to make sure that you are in the right frame of mind to trade. There is absolutely no shame in taking a break from trading if you are not in the right frame of mind. Trades that are made out of a sense of obligation, or that are absent-mindedly placed, will almost certainly end out-of-the-money. Make sure that you can dedicate the right amount of time and mental space to your trades every single time.

Final Mindset Checklist

Is My Broker Serving My Purpose

Many times, not wanting to trade or losing interest in trading is broker related and not trader related. If you feel like your broker platform is outdated, that their payout percentages are not consistent, or enough special features are not being made available to you, shop around. Long gone are the days of shady brokers offering platforms from offshore tax havens. Take the time to go through the list of accredited brokers, deciding which one fits best with your trading style and plan. With binary options now being well regulated, there is fierce competition within the market. If you feel like you would like something a little more from your broker, reach out and see what they can offer to assist you. Before moving brokers, make sure to check your local regulators' listings so you can avoid fraudulent or unregistered brokers. As long as you are taking your time to do the homework required, a broker move may be the best thing for bored or disinterested traders.

Are My Expectations in Check?

Never, and I do mean never, go into a trade with an expectation to profit. If you go into a trade with the expectation of winning x percentage of your trades, chances are you are going to end the trading day disappointed and frustrated. Do your homework, clear your mind of any expectations, and accept that losses are inevitable. Conduct your own reviews of what the market is doing for the day, and if you absolutely must, only factor in a 60% winning ratio on commodities options and around a 55% winning ratio on FOREX trades. The goal is always to tilt the odds in your favor, which means anything more than a 50%-win ratio is good.

Have Faith in Your Analysis

If you have gone through the relevant candlesticks and made use of the various analysis tools available to you, your mind should be at ease at your time of trade. If you are still having some doubts, make sure you go back and review your analysis. Fundamental analysis plays the most pivotal role in placing a trade and should never be glanced over or skipped. Be aware of what is happening in the world, schedule your trades accordingly, and trust the figures. If you still feel unsure of your trade, then do not trade at all. Knowledge is power in the binary options trading game. Keep perspective and make good decisions. Anything less than an informed trade is nothing more than gambling.

Be Focused

do not trade if you are distracted or not feeling like you can devote the right amount of time to your trades. Besides the fact that there are hundreds of asset types to choose from, the sheer volume of analytical and general tools required to make an informed trade will demand that you can remain focused on the task at hand. If you feel that your head is not entirely in the game, do not trade at all. If you feel you want to trade anyway, keep your premiums low and stick to assets you are familiar with. Always remember that while trend is your friend, trading when you cannot give the market your full attention is likely to end in a loss. Rather than forcing yourself to trade for the sake of it, be patient and wait for strong trends to immerse, or return to trading when your head is back in the game.

Stick to Your Trading Plan Always

Your trading plan is, and always will be, the most important aspect of binary trading options. You cannot begin analysis, nor can you choose a trade without first instituting your plan. When emotions start to mess with your trades, take a step away from the trading desk and reiterate what your trading goals are. According to professional and veteran traders, the only way to overcome emotions or irrational trading decisions is to create a plan that works for you and stick to it. While search engines may produce endless streams of ideas on how others accumulated wealth, these ideas do not necessarily apply to you. This is because every trader is different, and while the fundamentals of trading remain the same for everyone, trading plans are as unique as the trader.

If you are stuck on your own trading plan, you can find one that may work for you online and then tweak it as you develop and grow. But it is very important that you only trade on demo accounts while fine tuning someone else's plan to match your own unique trading style. Before you even begin trading, make sure you go over your trading plan, and reiterate that you will stick to this plan no matter what. Leave your ego and your emotions at the door when you enter the trading desk.

Practice Makes Perfect

While practicing on a demo account may not be a specific mental mindset, it does help you to put your mind at ease when you trade real money. Knowing that you have tried your strategies and plans, and tested your theories without having to ever lose real money gains you valuable experience. There are no trading shortcuts, and there is no substitute for experience when it comes to trading. Binary options trading is not an exception. do not be fooled by the simplicity of the trade placement. When starting your trading journey, or when changing your strategies, try to trade on your demo account with one-hour options. Take note of what times of the day are most consistent, when swings occur, and how well you react to market fluctuations. Luck does play a part in coming out in-the-money, but rational trade placements increase the chances of luck being on your side. As Louis Pasteur said, "chance favors only the prepared mind."

Always Manage Your Money

Nothing will get your emotions stirred up quite as quickly as losing money irresponsibly. While certain measures have been put in place by brokers and governing officials to curtail massive losses, it is still vital that you manage your own money and risk by yourself. No matter what the regulations are, if you are trading emotionally, you stand the chance to lose your entire investment. As much as brokers can restrict your trading by ensuring you are trading at the right level, losing a significant amount of money, especially on a single trade, will trigger an emotional spiral. A conservative trader should look at wagering 2% of their account balance. If, however, you feel that you are more aggressive in your trading style, you should wager up to 10%. As much as I understand that it can be frustrating initially to only trade in small amounts, this rule is in place to protect you from losing your entire account on a single trade. If you are riding the wave of a particularly strong trend, you may want to consider temporarily increasing this percentage, but be prepared for the higher risk. In the beginning stages of trading, make a conscious decision to not make use of double up or sell early options. Never ever increase your investment amount to try and offset a loss. This is the quickest way for trading to get into your mind and leave you as a broke casualty.

Have a Reputable Signal Provider?

As a beginner, you may not need a signal provider. But as you progress to becoming more experienced, or if you decide to trade full time, you will want to invest in a good alert or signal service provider. Placing your trust in these service providers prevents you from having to constantly check your trades, and keeps your mind clutter-free and available to work on your strategies. Make sure that your software provider is legitimate by checking customer reviews. Good bots or signal software rely on tested algorithms that indicate whether your asset is trending. Most bots do not work well in markets that are ranging, though. Make sure you validate your software winning percentages and do your due diligence.

Using brokers who offer to trade on our behalf is generally a bad idea. As an experienced trader, relying on unemotional software that is set to your prescribed parameters is a far more reliable bet. Remember, binary options brokers make money off of your losses too.

Put Your Mind at Rest with Correlating Assets

Your trading plan should include how many open positions, or active trades, you will have at any one time. To begin with, most traders cannot handle the pressure of more than three open positions. If you are trading options on the same asset, you may want to increase that number, but trading different assets that require you to check trends should not split your focus too much. You do not need to be at the trading desk at all times. Choose your trading hours and make a commitment to yourself that you will not allow trading to consume too much of your time or thoughts. If you have chosen to have multiple positions open at a time, you will need to make sure you have diversified these trades without correlations that work against your interest. An example of this would be gold and the Euro, which generally move in the opposite direction to the U.S. Dollar. Placing multiple positions incorrectly can lead to you feeling flustered and ultimately may end up with one order canceling out another. You would ultimately lose because of lower payoff ratios, ultimately causing frustration.

Always Expect to Lose

Finally, the last item on your mindset checklist is understanding that you have a 50% chance to lose your premium. Following all of the strategies, tips, and tricks in this book will certainly help you to level the playing field when it comes to trading binary options, but you cannot predict the future. Putting real money on the line to place a trade is a risk and the second you have placed that first trade, chances are you will begin to doubt everything you have learned and practiced. Going into a trade with the expectation that you will lose will help to calm your nerves and, because you have already resigned yourself to the fact that you will lose, those wins will feel all the more exciting.

Do not commit funds that you cannot afford. Even with all of your experience and knowledge, the chances of having a few first-time losses are pretty high. do not be tempted to trade with brokers who offer promotional bonuses on high deposits. The trading commitments that come with these promotions are usually valued at up to 30 times more than usual withdrawal limits. This means that you could be locked into keeping your money in your platform account for a considerable period of time before ever being able to access it. Here is the reality about trading bonuses; seven out of ten traders will fail to cash in on their bonuses. Be patient, do not rush, and do not put pressure on yourself to make huge amounts of money. Binary options are a long-term investment growth plan. Start small, only bid what you can afford, keep your mind in the game, and you will start to accumulate smaller gains that increase over time. do not be tempted into going against your money management plan. It just isn't worth it.

Options Strategies

Covered Call

The Covered Call strategy allows an investor to completely purchase the underlying asset. The investor must write and sell the call option immediately after the purchase of the same asset. The number of shares must be the same.

Example: (a)

Trader:

Buy:		Stock A	100 $10 ea.
Write + Sell:	Put: $10/stock	Stock A	100 Prem: $100

Profit So Far: $100

This technique is used by investors for their short-term trading practices and when they have a neutral view of the underlying asset. It is often used by traders who wish to secure their investment against any potential decrease in value. It's a decent simple plan to start with, and if you're concerned about missing out on a potential investment, then that's the way to go.

Married Put

The strategy of Married Put is used when investors are bullish about the price of the underlying asset. They buy the shares of the asset, and then buy the same number of shares at the same time. They do this to secure their investment against future short-term losses. It's a way to cash on an investment right now, so they don't have to worry about losing anything when things get rough. In a way, the scope for gains in this is infinite.

The married strategy is like an insurance policy that sets the floor price in the event of a dramatic decline in the price of the asset.

Example: (a)

Trader:

Buy:		Stock A	100	$10 ea.
	Put: $10/stock	Stock A	100	Prem: $100

Cost: $100

Bull Call Spread

The Bull Call Spread strategy is used when investors are optimistic about a particular asset and expect the price of the underlying asset to rise moderately.

They buy a call option at a certain strike price and then simultaneously write and sell a call option at a higher price. When prompted, the trader effectively buys a lower-priced asset, and at the same time, sells a higher-priced asset-and thus generates profit.

In order for this strategy to succeed, all call options must have the same underlying asset and the expiration month.

Example: (a)

Trader:

Buy:	Call: $10/stock	Stock B	100	Prem: $100
Write + Sell:	Call: $13/stock	Stock B	100	Prem: $100

Bear Put Spread

The Bear Put Spread strategy is used when investors are bay about the price of the underlying asset. In this scenario, they expect the price to fall further.

They buy a set option at a specific price, then write and sell another set option at a price lower than their first option. When asked, the trader effectively sells the higher-priced asset, then simultaneously re-purchases the lower-priced asset-and thus generates profit as well.

Like the bull call spread, this would only be effective if investors deal with the same asset on a similar expiry date. This strategy limits profit and, more importantly, loss.

Example: (a)

Trader:

Buy:	Put: $10/stock	Stock C	100	Prem: $100
Write + Sell:	Put: $7/stock	Stock C	100	Prem: $100

Protective Collar

The protective Collar strategy closes benefits without the need to sell the shares of the underlying asset. Investors purchase an out-of-the-money option, then write and sell an out-of-money call option. Again, this only works if investors deal with the same asset.

It is used by investors who have invested a long time in the underlying asset and gained dividends from it. If the price of the asset decreases, the option owned by Put will guarantee income. If the asset price increases, you'll make a profit once someone exercises your written call option.

Example: (a)

Trader: Stock D@$12

Buy: Put: $10/stock   Stock D   100 Prem: $100

Write + Sell: Call: $14/stock   Stock D   100 Prem: $100

Straddles

he Long Straddle strategy is mainly used to minimize losses and sustain profits. In this case, the loss is limited to the price of the options.

To be successful, investors must purchase a coupon and call option at the same price, the exact expiry date and the also exact underlying asset. They use this tactic when they feel that the price of the commodity is going to shift dramatically. However, they're not sure the path the price is going to take.

Example: (a)

Trader: Stock E@$10

Buy: Put: $10/stock   Stock E   100   Prem: $100

         Call: $10/stock   Stock E   100   Prem: $100

Strangles

The Long Strangle (not to be confused with the previous one) strategy is a cheaper strategy than the long straddle because the options are purchased out of money. It is used to restrict losses to the price of the call and put options. In addition, investors use this approach when they expect that the price of the underlying asset will move dramatically. However, they don't know which path the price is going to take.

To be successful, investors purchase both a fixed and a call option with the same asset and the same expiry date, but the prices of the options are different from each other. The strike price of the given option must be below the strike price of the call option. This way, all solutions would result in an out-of-the-money solution.

Example: (a)

Trader: Stock F@$10

Buy: Put: $9/stock   Stock F   100   Prem: $100

         Call: $12/stock   Stock F   100   Prem: $100

Log Call Butterfly Spread

The butterfly spread technique is a variation of the spread of the bear and the spread of the bull. It also uses a range of rates. A kind of butterfly spread strategy allows investors to purchase a call option at the lowest strike price. They then immediately write and sell two call options at a higher price and another call option at the cheapest possible price. So, if anyone exercises their written capacity, you exercise yours easily. You end up selling high and purchasing low-inducing benefits.

It is also possible for them to buy a put option at the highest price and then immediately write and sell two put options at a lower strike price while selling the last put option at the lowest strike price. So, if anyone exercises their written capacity, you exercise yours easily. Again, you end up selling high and buying low, thus, causing profit again.

Example: (a)

Trader A: Stock G@$10

Buy:	Call: $10/stock	Stock G	100	Prem: $100
Write + Sell:	Call: $13/stock	Stock G	100	Prem: $100
	Call: $14/stock	Stock G	100	Prem: $100
	Call: $16/stock	Stock G	100	Prem: $100

Trader B:	Stock G@$10			

Buy:	Put: $10/stock	Stock G	100	Prem: $100
Write + Sell:	Put: $8/stock	Stock G	100	Prem: $100
	Put: $7/stock	Stock G	100	Prem: $100
	Put: $5/stock	Stock G	100	Prem: $100

Iron Condor

The strategy of the Iron Condor is difficult to execute. It's not about new options for investors, but it takes a lot of time and practice to be successful. Investors have both a short and a long place in two kinds of strangling strategies: a bearish and a bullish direction.

But no matter which way, if anyone exercises your written choice, you exercise yours quickly. Done right, you end up selling high and buying low, inducing profit again.

Try not to confuse the strike prices by using this option technique. You can still end up purchasing less and selling higher.

Trader:	Stock H@$10			

Write + Sell:	Put: $9/stock	Stock H	100	Prem: $100
Buy:	Put: $8/stock	Stock H	100	Prem: $100
Write + Sell:	Call: $12/stock	Stock H	100	Prem: $100

Buy: Call: $14/stock Stock H 100 Prem: $100

Iron Butterfly

The Iron Butterfly incorporates a short or long straddle with a strangler. It's sort of the same as the butterfly spreads. The difference, however, is that an iron butterfly uses both a set and a call option simultaneously. This technique limits losses and profits to a certain degree. Investors ensure that risks are reduced, and that risk is restricted by the use of out-of-the-money options.

Trader: Stock I@$10

Buy: Put: $9/stock Stock I 100 Prem: $100 Out of the money

Write + Sell: Put: $11/stock Stock I 100 Prem: $100 In the money

Write + Sell: Call: $9/stock Stock I 100 Prem: $100 In the money

Buy: Call: $12/stock Stock I 100 Prem: $100 Out of the money

Currency Options

What Is a Currency Option?

The currency option (also known as the Forex option) is a contract that gives the purchaser the right but not the obligation to purchase or sell a specific currency at a specified exchange rate at or before a given date. A fee is charged to the seller for this right.

Currency options are one of the most prevalent ways for businesses, individuals, and financial institutions to avoid adverse currency fluctuation.

Basics of Currency Options

By buying a currency put or call, investors may hedge from the risk of foreign currency. Currency options are derivatives dependent on the currency pairs underlying them. Trading options for currency include a range of strategies for use in forex markets. The strategy used by a trader depends in large part on the type of option and the broker or platform it is offered. In competitive forex markets, the characteristics of options differ much more widely than in more regulated stock and futures exchanges.

For several reasons, traders like to swap currency options. They can only lose the premium they pay to purchase the options, but they have infinite upside potential. Some traders use FX options to hedge open positions in the forex cash market. The cash market, also known as the physical market or the spot market, is the direct settlement of goods and securities transactions, as opposed to the futures market. Traders like the trading of options because this gives them the opportunity to trade and benefit from the forecast of the market direction on the basis of economic, political, or other news.

However, the premium on trading contracts for currency options can be quite high. The premium depends on the price and expiry date of the attack. They cannot be re-traded or sold once you purchase an options contract. The trading of forex options is complicated and has several moving components, making it difficult to assess their value. The risks include interest-rate differentials (IRDs), market volatility, the expiry time horizon, and the current currency pair prices.

Vanilla Options Basics

Two key options, calls and puts are open.

The holder of a call option has the right (but not the obligation) to acquire the asset for a given period of time at a predetermined price (the strike price). If the stock does not meet the strike price before the expiry date, the option ends and is valuable. Investors buy telephone calls if they believe that the share price of the underlying security will increase or sell a call if they think it will fall. The selling of an option is also known as "writing" an option.

The holder of a put option can sell an underlying asset at a predetermined price.

The seller (or author) of the put option, must purchase the shares at the strike price. You can exercise options at any time before the option expires.

Investors buy posts if they think the underlying stock's share price will fall, or if they think it will, though, they sell one. Put buyers—those with a "long" position—either are speculative purchasers looking for leverage or insurance purchasers, seeking to secure their long stock positions for an option-set period. Salespersons keep a 'short' in anticipation that the demand will go up (or remain stable at least) A worst-case scenario for a put vendor is a downward trend. The maximum profit will be proportional to the premium received and will be realized when the underlying price is at or above the strike price of the option at the expiry. The maximum loss for an exposed writer is indefinite.

Trade will still require a long currency and a short currency pair. In essence, the buyer must say how much they want to purchase, the price at which they want to buy, and the expiry date. A seller then addresses the trade with a quoted premium. Common choices may have expirations in American or European models. Traders are entitled to put-and-call options, but there is no responsibility. When the current exchange rate takes the money (OTM) options out, they will expire without interest.

SPOT Options

An exotic alternative used for trading currencies involves the trading of single payment options (SPOT). Spot options have higher premium costs than conventional options, but can be set and implemented easier. A currency trader buys a SPOT option when entering a scenario (for example, "I assume that EUR/USD will settle above 1.5205 15 days."), and an award is quoted.

If this option is bought by the buyer, the put immediately pays out if the situation happens. In essence, the option is transformed into cash automatically.

The SPOT is a financial product with a contract structure more flexible than conventional alternatives. This strategy is all or nothing and is also known as binary or digital options. The buyer will be selling a scenario like EUR/USD in 12 days, which will hit 1, 3000. We offer premium quotations, which are paid on the basis of the probability of the occurrence. If this event occurs, the buyer will benefit. If this does not occur, the premium paid by the buyer will be forfeited. contracts require a higher premium than standard options. SPOT contracts can also be written to compensate whether they reach a particular point, a number of specific points, or do not meet a particular point. Naturally, the premium requirements for different choice arrangements will be higher.

Exotic options with features such as a barrier option, a binary option, a digital option, or a lookback option, for example, add more to the payoff than the value of the underlying instrument maturity.

Example of a Currency Option

Let's say an investor is bullish about the euro and believes that the US dollar will rise. The buyer acquires a currency call option for the euro at a hard price of $115 because currency premiums are 100 times the exchange rate. If the buyer buys the deal, the euro spot rate is $110. Assume that the spot price of the euro at the expiry date is $118. The currency option is then stated to have expired in the capital. Consequently, the investor's income is $300 or (100) × ($118–$115) less than the premium paid for the currency call.

Basics of Day Trading Strategies

Day trading is a difficult occupation in which one carries out purchase and sale simultaneously. Amateur traders carry out buying and selling of securities on a purchase-day in order to make profit from short-term price fluctuations. Day traders use different methods of analysis such as technical analysis.

What is a day?

By definition, a day is 24 hours. For this reason, the system of buying and selling securities in the same day is based on this time period.

How to Day trade? [the process of buying and selling at the same time]

The first thing you need to do when you decide to day trade is decided on whether or not you can actually do it. The truth is that some people feel more comfortable buying and selling at the same time than others, so some may feel more confident in doing it than others. But this doesn't mean that you don't have to put in some effort and try your best so you can make money with trading if possible.

It is not uncommon for people who day trade to be unable to ever make more than $5-$10 a day. However, that doesn't mean that is has to stay this way. There are plenty of days when you can make more than $10, even more than $100. It will require some time and work (which most people are used to), but if you can make it happen, go for it.

What is the best way to buy and sell at the same time?

There are two approaches to this: one with low risk and the other with high danger. With the first method, you only need to buy when the price goes down and sell when it goes up. This is not a bad method to use, but it does have a high risk involved. You have to use a broker which offers

CFD trading so you can actually close them in case your trades lose money.

With the second method, you don't have any risk in buying or selling at the same time. However, this means that you will spend a lot of time trying to make trades that will turn out for you or against you.

Day trading involves finding candlestick patterns that occur every day. You can use many online tools to do this. You can also look for related news on the stock before making the trade. And you will need to be up-to-date with what is happening in the market at all times.

One thing you should remember when day trading is that it is quite easy for newcomers to make mistakes because they aren't well-informed; therefore, they often get their trades wrong and lose money. This shouldn't discourage you, though, because once you start gathering experience, getting the right trade will become easier for you.

The System

Setting up a system is also important when it comes to day trading because you will have many different trades that happen every single day. You should have a systematic method in place so you can make sure you are making the right trade. The point is, if you are making more mistakes than wins, then it won't matter whether or not your system works because even your best trading plan can get you 99.9% of your trades wrong! As I said before, this is no big deal, though; if you rely on the same plan for years and years, then one extra percent can mean quite a lot in the end.

If you want to make the system work, then you should follow the basics. You will need to go over all of your trades and see if they can be done with a different way of trading. You should try to figure out why the trade failed and learn from it. If this isn't done, then your trading record will always be less than impressive!

How does Day Trading Work? [the process of buying and selling at the same time]

How do you buy and sell at the same time? The name of the game is to buy low and sell high. If you do this, then you will always make money. This is because the price of the stock will go up if you sell it after buying at a low price and that is when you can make money!

You can also look for successful traders on social media to see what they are doing. They might even be willing to mentor you and show you how to accomplish it because learning from successful individuals is far superior to learning on your own!

Once again, don't jump into anything right away. Take your time and learn as much as possible about day trading. Also, don't start your career before you are ready because it won't be easy to make money in the beginning! Just start out if you are really confident that you can do it because day trading is not something to be taken lightly!

Day trading is a high-risk occupation which requires great discipline to become successful. Hence, you have to have a proper strategy in place so you can make money with day trading!

Conclusion

Option strategies can be grouped into two main categories: directional and non-directional.

A directional strategy is a strategy that benefits from a rise or drop in the price of the underlying stock.

While there are many different directional strategies, they can primarily be separated into two categories: put buying and call buying. Put buying refers to the option of "buying to open" (BTO) a put option on a stock, while call buying refers to BTO on a call option.

A non-directional strategy benefits when the price stays precisely the same in either direction, meaning both up or down price movements are neutralized. These are typically credit spreads.

A credit spread is a strategy of buying two option contracts for an asset with different strike prices but with the same expiration date. Typically, this is done by purchasing a call option with a high strike price and selling to open a call option with a lower strike price, or vice versa for put credit spreads. Below is a diagram that depicts the differences between these two types of credit spreads.

Example:

Let's say you buy to open 10 contracts on XYZ stock. If you're optimistic about the stock, you will buy 10 calls with a strike price of $15 that expire in January 2020. If you are bearish, you will buy 10 puts at the $10 strike price.

Why does this work? If XYZ stock is above $15 at the expiration of the option contract, the $15 strike price will be in-the-money (ITM), and all 10 of your BTO calls will be worth at least their intrinsic value (IV). The

$10 strike price is out-of-the-money (OTM) and therefore worthless, so you can buy back these contracts for an immediate profit of your initial premium.

If XYZ stock is below $10 at expiration, both the BTO calls would be out-of-the-money (OTM), which means they are worthless. The $10 call would be ITM and worth at least its intrinsic value (IV). The BTO puts would be useless, so you can repurchase them for their premium.

If XYZ stock is above $15 at expiration, all 10 of your BTO calls will be worth at least their IV. Where is the value in buying 10 BTO puts? They are both OTM, meaning they are worthless. Where is the value in buying 10 BTO calls? They are both ITM and both worth more than their IV.

Bargain Hunting:

The purpose of this strategy is to find stocks that are highly volatile yet undervalued by the market.

This is the lowest possible risk portfolio with the best possible reward, and it's a common strategy for beginners. But, of course, if you're still learning about and investing in options and aren't familiar with stock analysis or technical analysis, then this strategy might not be the best thing for you.

The main reason why this portfolio works is that you use a combination of long-term fundamentals and short-term technical analysis to determine which stocks are undervalued or overvalued.

Support my work

Thank you for reading this book. I hope you are now more familiar with the world of options and online trading.

If you have the pleasure to support and spread my work, then I invite you to leave a review on Amazon.

Frame with your smartphone this QR code and review this book.

Thank you